Life His
SHIRDI S

C000245473

Life History of Shirdi Sai Baba was originally written in Telugu by Ammula Sambasiva Rao, and translated into English by Thota Bhaskara Rao. The book delves deep into the details of the life of Shirdi Sai Baba right from his birth till his attainment of *Samadhi*.

The author has expounded *Sai Tatwa* or Sai philosophy in a simple language, interspersed with engrossing anecdotes in the life of Sai devotees.

Ammula Sambasiva Rao, an ardent Sai devotee, has done pioneering work for the spread of Sai philosophy and Sai awakening in the people of Andhra Pradesh. He has undertaken the performance of a unique yagna *called "Sri Sai Koti Nama Likitha Maha Yagna" in Sai temples in Andhra Pradesh, and other places in India. He is the Founder-President of the Shree Shirdi Sai Baba Seva Ashram, a registered body with its headquarters at Hyderabad.*

Sri Sambasiva Rao has written several books in Telugu on Sai philosophy and the life history of Sai Baba.

Books by Ammula Sambasiva Rao

Sai Kiran Series books are in Telugu only.

1. Shirdi Aaratulu
2. Shirdi Sai Sukthulu (Sayings of Shirdi Sai)
3. Sai Baba Yevaru? (Who is Sai Baba?)
4. Sai Baba nu Yenduku Poojinchali? (Why to Worship Sai Baba)
5. Sai Maargam (The Path Shown by Sai Baba)
6. Sai Sainyam (Sai's Army)
7. Sai Avataralu (Incarnations of Sai Baba)
8. Shri Shirdi Sai Baba Jeevita Charitramu (The Life History of Sri Shirdi Sai Baba)
9. Saitho na Anubhavalu (My Experiences with Sai)
10. Shri Shirdi Sai Baba Vrata Vidhanamu (Shri Shirdi Sai Baba's Vratam - Mode of Worship)

Published by
Sterling Publishers Private Limited

LIFE HISTORY OF SHIRDI SAI BABA

AMMULA SAMBASIVA RAO

English translation by
THOTA BHASKARA RAO

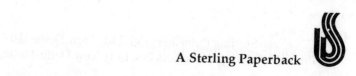

A Sterling Paperback

STERLING PAPERBACKS
An imprint of
Sterling Publishers (P) Ltd.
A-59 Okhla Industrial Area, Phase-II,
New Delhi-110020.
Tel: 26387070, 26386209; Fax: 91-11-26383788
E-mail: ghai@nde.vsnl.net.in
www.sterlingpublishers.com

Life History of Shirdi Sai Baba
© 1997, Ammula Sambasiva Rao
ISBN 81 207 2033 4
Reprint 1998, 1999, 2000, 2002, 2003
Reprint 2004, 2005, 2006, 2007

All rights are reserved. No part of this publication may be reproduced, stored in a retrieval system or transmitted, in any form or by any means, mechanical, photocopying, recording or otherwise, without prior written permission of the original publisher.

Published by Sterling Publishers Pvt. Ltd., New Delhi-110 020.
Printed at Sterling Publishers Pvt. Ltd., New Delhi-110020.

AUTHOR'S PREFACE
(for the first Telugu Edition)

To write the life history of Shri Shirdi Sai Baba is really a bold act. It is because there is none till now who knows fully the greatness of Baba. There will not be one in future also. Our publisher at Shirdi decided to get the *Life History of Sai Baba* written by me. This was an opportunity given to me by Sai indirectly. I commenced writing on 8 March 1993 sitting in Baba's house, Dwarakamai, Shirdi. The printing of the first edition started on the Telugu New Year day (Ugadi day) on 24 March 1993. On the same day Baba made me undertake "Sree Sai Koti Nama Likitha Maha Yagna", at Machilipatnam in Andhra Pradesh. In this *yagna,* Baba's name "Sree Sai" written three crores and fifty lakhs times by the Sai devotees were offered to him at the Sai Dhyan Mandir under construction by Shri Abdul Rahim. The *yagna* started with a procession and while it was proceeding towards the Sai Dhyan Mandir, the printing of the first edition of the *Life History* commenced at Secunderabad. After that, the printing was resumed only after 5 April 1993. From that day the writing and printing were done without break and completed on 12 May 1993.

From the time I started writing this book, I had tremendous pressures in my profession. I had to work daily from 8 a.m. to 8 p.m.. After coming home at night I had to continue the writing of this book. To add to this, the Sai *pujas* and Sai *vratams* performed in the houses of Sai devotees, on holidays had increased considerably during this period. Some days I used to feel physically and mentally weak to continue with the writing, because of the increase in the Sai *puja* activities during the day. When I tried to postpone the writing to the next day due to fatigue, Baba punished me be hitting me with a whip. As there was no other alternative, I used to write enough pages sufficient for the next day's printing and then go to sleep. I can never forget the tests I was subjected to during this period. On one side there was the restless job and on the other side Baba with his whip. My body became weak and exhausted. I felt sleepy and the mind craved for rest. Whatever might be my state, Baba never left me until I completed the writing of the material required for the next day's printing. I feared to look at my condition. But, there were a number of *leelas* and miracles shown to me by him during this period. There were a number of occasions when Baba directed me to write in a particular manner. He has shown me some of his life's incidents in my dreams. In the last it appeared that the writing was according to Sai Baba's thinking and not as I desired it to be.

I feared attending office in the day, because of tremendous pressure of work. I also feared going home in the nights, because of the punishment Baba would give me. If Baba found my mind going astray, he used the whip. If my mind went after some item, Baba destroyed that item. I had to fully concentrate on writing this book. It was a strange experience, the affectionate punishment given to me by Baba. The more he punished me, the more determination I developed. I felt that I deserved that punishment. I also felt that it was necessary for me. In this way Sai Baba was always present behind me and guided me in my writing. For this I am offering my prostrations to Sai. If he had not been present behind me and guided me, it would not have been possible to write and publish this in only 38 days.

Some Sai devotees may say after reading this book, that they never read or heard certain matters contained in this book and is therefore irrelevant. But it is my humble submission that I have incorporated only those matters as conveyed to me by Sai with not even a single item written by imagination or exaggerated. Whatever was conveyed to me by Sai, I have tried to include in this book. When I sat in the Dwarakamai on 8 March 1993 and commenced writing this book, I prayed to Baba on the following matters:

1) I will never approach anyone for material for writing the Life History of Baba. I will not run here and there. Only Baba should convey to me the details of his life story, to enable me to write correctly.
2) Baba should ensure that only the facts that took place during his lifetime, should find place in the present *Life History.* Untrue and irrelavent matters should find no place.

I sincerely believe that Baba heard my prayer and fulfilled my two wishes completely. In several instances when I had to write small stories, I have given the moral which has to be learnt, at the end of the story, at the instance of Baba, who induced it in my mind. Till then I did not understand the actual moral in the story. This was purely due to Baba's grace only. After holding the pen in my hand, I felt that my intellect and mind were no more under my control but in Baba's custody. In such strange circumstances, my body was used by Sai to write the *Life History* and I am always indebted to him.

I fully believe that those who read this *Life History* with complete devotion, regularly, will derive the corresponding benefits. I request the readers of this book to convery their views or experiences to me.

If the books are published and distributed by voluntary organisations, the cost of the book will be very less. But if the same is done by the commercial establishments, the main consideration will be profit and the sales of the book will depend on the profit. Devotion and business are two separate aspects. Therefore, I have fixed the cost of the book with the permission of Baba. I have no desire to earn money through sales of this book. What is required is "Sai's

Grace". If it is there I know there will be more than the required money in the house.

I am placing this book on the *Samadhi* of Sai Baba at Shirdi and with deep sense of gratitude I am dedicating this to him for having been with me like a shadow and making me finish this book.

This *Life History* is that of 'Yogiraj' and 'Rajadhiraj'. Shirdi Sai Baba and all those associated with the production, distribution, sales and transport, etc., of this book and also those who do 'Parayana' of this book, will have the protection of Sai Baba throughout their lives and this is my prayer to Sai Baba.

Now the devout readers should join with us and in the name of Sai, speak out certain wishes to those devotees who do 'Parayana' of the *Life History*.

1) Let there be complete peace of mind to those who do 'Parayan' with devotion and sincerity.
2) Let their wishes be fulfilled.
3) Let their sufferings be over.
4) Let Sai Baba be their 'Sadguru' and take them in the righteous path.
5) Let the worldy desires be removed from those who frequently do Parayana of the Life History.
6) Let there be peace and happiness for all.
7) Let Sai baba be bound by the above assurances given by us to the readers.

Camp: Shirdi 01.06.1993 (Bakrid) **Ammula Sambasiva Rao**
Flat No. G/E, Geervani Apartments
13/89, Sanjaynagar, Malkajgiri,
HYDERABAD - 500 047

JAI SAI RAM—JAI JAI SAI RAM

TRANSLATOR'S PREFACE

Om Sree Ganeshaya - Namaha

My salutations to the lotus feet of the Samardha Sadguru Shri Shirdi Sai Baba.

My salutations to Pujya Sri Ammula Sambasiva Raoji, the author of the *Life History of Shri Shirdi Sai Baba* in Telugu.

Strange are the ways of Sai Baba in dragging his devotees not only to him but also to his trusted messengers who have dedicated themselves to the spread of *Sai Tatwa* or Sai philosophy all over the length and breadth of our sacred motherland.

I have been a devotee a Sai Baba of Shirdi for three decades. While the late Sri B.V. Narasimha Swamiji of Madras was responsible for the spread of Sai philosophy in the South, through his great writings about Sai Baba and establishing All India Sai Samaj, I find Poojya Sri Ammula Sambasiva Raoji doing pioneering work for the spread of Sai philosophy and Sai awakening in the people of Andhra Pradesh, mainly. I say 'mainly' because of late, his activities are spreading not only to the neighbouring States of Andhra Pradesh but also to distant places like Jaipur in Rajasthan, New Delhi and Kharagpur. Before proceeding to give an account of his activities connected with the propogation of Sai philosophy, I would like to tell the readers, briefly about my acquaintance with this great person, who is now 'Guruji' to thousands and thousands of Sai devotees.

After my retirement from Government service in the year 1991, I longed to do service to Sai Baba by associating myself with a person doing selfless service in spreading Sai's message. At that time Pujya Sri Ammula Sambasiva Raoji was working as an Officer in the State Bank of India, Secunderabad. Knowing my desire, a friend of mine, Sri G. Manohar Babu who was also working in the same bank, introduced me to Sri Sambasiva Raoji.

We were attracted to each other from the very moment of my introduction to him. I used to attend the noon *Arathis* to Sai Baba in the makeshift Sai Baba Mandir set up by Sri Sambasiva Raoji inside the bank premises. I thanked Baba for having sent me to this great and simple person. I used to accompany Sri Sambasiva Raoji (hereinafter referred to as 'Guruji') for the conduct of Sai pujas and Sai *vratams* (observance of fast) in the houses of Sai devotees in the twin cities of Hyderabad and Secunderabad and sometimes in nearby districts, during holidays and sometimes after office hours. All the services rendered were absolutely free of cost. Till to this day Guruji had performed more than one thousand Sai *vratams.*

Guruji had also undertaken the performance of a unique *yagna* called "Sri Sai Koti Nama Likitha Maha Yagna" in Sai Baba temple at several places in Andhra Pradesh and also at Shirdi, Jaipur (Rajasthan) and New Delhi. In each *yagna* two crores of "Sree Sai" names written by the Sai devotees in the books supplied to them free of cost, are being put in specially constructed stupas in the Sai temples. Till date 35 such *yagnas* were conducted and the details are furnished elsewhere in this book. His speeches about Sai Baba and the way he expounds Baba's philosophy in the Satsang in simple words is a rare experience for the listeners.

Guruji has since resigned his job as an officer in the State Bank of India, so that he can be in the service of Sai Baba all the twenty-four hours and work for the establishment of 'Sai Yuga'. No sacrifice is too great in the service of Sai Baba.

Guruji has established "Shree Shirdi Sai Baba Seva Ashram" which is a registered body. He is the Founder -

President with headquarters at Hyderabad. Units of this parent body have been constituted at six different places in Andhra Pradesh till now. The important aims of these units are to spread the message of Shirdi Sai Baba among the general public in order to secure peace and harmony to mankind and to establish *ashrams* at different centres to facilitate Aadhyatmic Training Classes for different age groups.

Besides the above mentioned activities, Guruji has written several books in Telugu about Sai philosophy and the *Life History of Shirdi Sai Baba.* The circumstances under which this book was written and published were given in Guruji's (Author's) foreword. This *Life History* contains certain details which cannot be found in other similar publications.

The need to translate this *Life History of Shirdi Sai Baba* into other Indian languages was felt with the spread of Guruji's activities to other States of India. Hence, he has taken a decision to have the English and Hindi translations of the *Life History,* to start with.

Guruji had been asking me to take up the translation into English since sometime, but I was hesitating and postponing as I doubted my capacity to undertake such a work, that too connected with Sai Baba. But he finally told me in the last week of December, 1995, that I should commence the work from 1 January 1996, under any circumstances, and Sai Baba is there to give me necessary guidance.

Therefore with the blessings of Guruji and reposing full confidence in Sai Baba, I commenced the translation on 1 January 1996 as per the directions of Guruji, and completed the work on 14 February 1996, the day on which Guruji left for Kharagpur.

While I was writing the English translation of *Life History,* Sai Baba showed his *leela* as follows. The manuscript of the work came to nearly 500 pages in long hand and I was searching for a person who could type the matter correctly. I contacted several typewriting coaching institutes, where such work was done. But they were not prepared to undertake this work and those who were prepared, demanded huge sums. Samardha Sadguru Sai Baba came to my rescue in the form of Jagannadha Rao, a typist by profession, a Sai devotee and a complete stranger to me, who volunteered to do the typing, after knowing that the original work in Telugu was written by Pujya Sri Ammula Sambasiva Rao. He told me that he had heard the name and activities of Guruji and expressed his gratefulness for being of some service to him. He did the typing work with great devotion and promptness.

I pray to Sai Baba to shower his blessings on Sri Jagannadha Rao. If the above incident is not Sai Leela, what else it is?

I express my deep sense of gratitude to Sai Maharaj and also to Guruji for having given me the opportunity to be of real service to them and also for getting myself enlightened about 'Sai Avatar'.

Thota Bhaskara Rao

Jai Sai Ram
Om Sree Sainathaya Namaha!

SHRI SHIRDI SAI BABA'S ASSURANCES TO HIS DEVOTEES

1. Entry into Shirdi removes all sufferings.
2. Whether sufferers or very poor people, the moment they enter Dwarakamai, they will have happiness and wealth.
3. Even after leaving my physical body, I am very ever alert to the needs of my devotees.
4. The protection to my devotees will come from my Samadhi.
5. From my Samadhi itself, I will discharge all my duties.
6. My human body will speak from my Samadhi.
7. It is my duty to protect my devotees who come to me and who seek refuge in me.
8. My blessings are there to those who look to me.
9. Put your burdens on me and I shall carry them.
10. I shall give my advise or help the moment it is sought.
11. There is no question of 'Want' in the houses of my devotees.

THE METHOD OF DOING 'PARAYANA'
(DEVOTIONAL READING)

Parayan of the life history of Sai Baba can be done in two ways.

1) **NITYA PARAYANA** (Daily Parayana)
All the members of the family to sit at one place. A photo of Baba may be placed at a slightly elevated place and incense sticks burnt. According to the time that can be spared, the chapters in the book can be read. One among them can read out loudly while others hear it. There is no prescribed number of chapters to be read in this manner. It can be done according to their convenience. Before closing the Parayana every day, *camphor arathi* should be given to Baba's photo.

2) **SAPTAHA PARAYANA** (Making Parayana for One Week)
Those who want to do *Parayana* as a *Diksha* (as a vow) should commence on a Thursday and end it on the following Thursday. The number of chapters to be read is indicated in the Index Abstract. The *Saptaha Parayana* is to be done individually. The Parayana is to be done sitting before Baba's photo in the puja room. Now and then they should look into Baba's eyes and greet him. At the end of each day's *Parayana, camphor arathi* is to be given to Baba. After completion of the *Saptaha Parayana* an amount of Rs. 5 should be sent to Baba as *Guru Dakshina,* to the Shirdi address given below, through money order written in English. If possible, one or two poor people may be fed.

Sri Shirdi Sai Baba Samsthan
Shirdi P.O., Kopargaon Tq.
Ahmednagar District, Maharashtra - 423 109

Contents

FIRST DAY'S PARAYAN
THURSDAY

CHAPTER 1

The earth is only a small planet in this great Universe which is beyond the grasp of human intelligence. On this planet earth, there are numerous rivers, mountains, forests and oceans. Out of 84 million kinds of insects, birds and animals and other living creatures on this planet great sages have concluded that the humans are the best living forms who can lead a very high form of divine life. But they, without realising their higher form among the living beings, fell prey to arrogance, egoism and *agnana* (ignorance) with the result there is no peace for them, putting the entire creation to chaos and confusion. What is the cause for all this? We must know the answer for this in the first instance. Going further to know the evolution of life forms on this earth, we come to learn that life first started under the water. Later on, the creatures living under water learnt to live outside the water, i.e., on the earth also. Further evolution took place and creatures that can live on earth alone developed. Out of these creatures and animals developed the human form and finally man came into existence.

According to the above mentioned theory of evolution only, the order of Dashavatharas is determined in the *Puranas*. Firstly, Matsyavatara (In the form of fish) — Fish can live under water only. Then Kurmavatara (in the form of tortoise), which can live inside water as well as outside water, i.e., earth. Then Varahavatara, Narasimhavatara, Vamanavatara, etc. The Ramavatara and Krishnavatara have shown to what divine heights man can reach.

If we examine carefully the order of the Dashavatharas you find that there is no difference between this order and the theory of evolution of man. This theory of evolution establishes that life at first started under water, then slowly spread to the earth adopting itself to the climatic conditions of the earth. These creatures slowly developed into animal forms and man has also developed from animal.

Man is superior from other forms of animals, inasmuch as he is endowed with thinking power. He has established a social order in the society where everyone can live happily. Toward this end, certain social orders and regulations have started to come into being. People living in different parts of the earth have formulated their own set of social orders depending on the local conditions. Over a period, these social orders and regulations have strengthened and become the "religion" of those people.

People started strengthening their religions. The powerful among them became leaders and rulers. Religions started bowing before the powerful and a situation came when the religions had to toe the line of the powerful. Under religious banners, powerful rulers started invading other countries as well as attacking other religions also. This is the naked truth which is revealed by World History.

Thus, many religions started coming into our country 'Bharat'. Several foreign countries invaded our motherland and started spreading their religions here. Thus Christianity and Islam entered and established themselves. Religion is meant for leading an orderly and disciplined way of life in the society and nothing else. But towards the end of the twentieth century in our country also, several attrocities are being committed in the name of religion by certain religious fanatics or fundamentalists, considering today the country's political scenario — this should be carefully noted by all Sai Bhaktas. Though religion is good for the spiritual advancement, only peaceful methods should be followed as per our Hindu dharma. In the present day conditions, though it is desirable to have one religion for one country, the 'means' adopted to achieve this should be through 'Love' or *prema marga* only. We will try to know more about this as we proceed further.

India has been described by our ancestors as *Punya Bhoomi, Karma Bhoomi, Dharma Bhoomi,* and so on. We will now make an attempt to know how these names were given. Our country's history of the mid-18th century reveals how during the British rule, our ancient civilisation gradually adopted the modern ways of British civilisation. Under such circumstances, the Adi Devtas (celestial beings), Ashta Dikpalakas who guard our Punya Bhoomi, along with Bhoodevi (goldess of earth) went to Vishnu and narrated their woes to him as follows.

"All through the ages, we have been happily discharging the duties allotted by you in Bharata Desha. But under the changed circumstances the people are preferring happiness to dharma, wealth to justice, strength to love, bodily happiness to sacrifice, materialism to Godliness. Unless these undesirable qualities are nipped in the bud, it will lead to utter chaos in the near future. So you must take Avatar again in this world, to set things right as you have done during your Krishna Avatar in Dwaparayuga and established peace after the Maha Kurukshetra war." After hearing their appeal, Lord Vishnu replied as follows:

"All of you have discharged your duties properly and established peace, prosperity and happiness in Bharata Desha all these ages. But as soon as I finished my Krishna Avatar, Kali entered the earth. Adishakti has created this Kali with a purpose and therefore it is not proper to stop him from doing his work. The changes that you are noticing in the people of Bharata Desha are only due to this Kali."

Then they asked Lord Vishnu as to how to save the people from the actions of Kali and Lord Vishnu answered them as follows:

"You all know why Bharata Desha is called Punya Bhoomi. There are a number of places on earth, with heavy snowfalls and cold waves. There are several places where you cannot get water for drinking or proper food. There are other places which are very hot. But only in places like Bharata Desha, there are different seasons. There are also a number of life giving rivers. Therefore, the people are able to raise good crops and are happy. They are able to take bath regularly and conduct divine activities. The Wind-God gives good air. Only those who are lucky and did good in previous births are born in this Punya Bhoomi and enjoy their natural happiness. This is briefly the history of this Punya Bhoomi." Lord Vishnu continued. "Kali came later to our country after showing his effects in other parts of this planet. His effects will be intensified in the near future and then the people of this country also will be subject to a lot of changes.

"Importance to one's duties will take a back seat while importance to wealth will increase. Everyone desires that others should work for him. But the fruits will be enjoyed by him only. This leads to class conflicts. In the name of religion, caste, regions and also sex, people will form into groups and will shed blood. Morals will disappear. People belonging to different religions will pray to their respective gods but none will follow the teachings of gods. Worship will be mechanical and devotion and worship will be separated. Opportunists will steal God's wealth also. It is difficult to save mankind from such effects of Kali. This is Yuga Dharma. Slowly pious and sincere actions will disappear and there will not be any connection between the thoughts and words; deeds wil. also be entirely different.

"It is impossible to save such a situation completely from the influence of Kali. But to a certain extent it can be checked and brought to a balance with dharma. I am the preserver of this world. My work increases with the selfishness of man. Therefore, I advise you to approach 'Lord Shiva' and put forth your prayers. Then he will come down to this world in the form of Datta Avatar and will impart 'Jnana' for mankind and will establish peace by his teachings." Thereupon the Adi Devatas, Ashta Dikpalakas and Bhoodevi approached Lord Shiva and put forth their woes. Accepting their pleas he promised that he would very shortly come to Bharata Desha as Datta Avatar. But since it is Kaliyug, where people are more materialistic, he will show more miracles after leaving the physical body than when he is with the body. Thus assured, by Lord Shiva, they come back to their respective places in this world and await eagerly for the birth of Lord Shiva.

As per his promise, Lord Shiva was waiting for an opportune time and for pious parents to whom he would be born on this planet earth.

"Jnana Swarupa Sai Saranam"

CHAPTER 2

When our country was under foreign domination, the State of the Nizam with Hyderabad as his capital extended up to Aurangabad, presently in Maharashtra State.

In this State there is a small village named Patri, situated among green fields, trees and other natural settings and taking the villagers to divine heights.

The water flowing in the rivulet adjoining this village had the effects of the water from river Ganga, curing several ailments. In this village there lived a pious couple named Ganga Bhavajya and Devagiri Amma. They led a happy and contented life. They did not have any property worth the name.

Ganga Bhavajya used to ferry a boat in the adjoining river and lived on this meagre earnings. Though they were poor in terms of wealth, they were contented, tolerant, tactful and had peace, Ganga Bhavajya used to worship Lord Shiva and Devagiri Amma used to worship Gowri Devi. Under any circumstances, the worship of Lord Shiva and Gowri Devi would be done before the couple attended to other items of work for they believed that there was divine presence in their house, protecting them every moment. But sadly they were not blessed with children. So they used to pray to Shiva and Parvathi to bless them with children.

One day in Kailash, Shiva told Parvathi that the time for him to take birth on earth had come as promised to Bhoodevi. Then Parvathi pleaded with Lord Shiva that she be allowed to take birth on earth and assist Shiva in his

Avatar. But he did not agree, that in his new Avatar, he proposed to practise strictly what he intended to preach and Parvathi would have no role to play in his 'Fakir' life. He then showed Parvathi, Ganga Bhavajya and Devagiri Amma on the earth, telling her that they are the couple to whom he would be born. Then Parvathi said that since she would not take birth on earth along with Lord Shiva, they should visit Ganga Bhavajya and Devagiri Amma now. He agreed and in the first instance sent Ganga Devi to fill Patri village and its surroundings with water. There was a heavy downpour, inundating the village and surroundings. Fearing that the boats would be washed away in the floods, Ganga Bhavajya proceeded to the nearby river to take care of the boats after taking his night meal.

At about 9.00 p.m. in the night, there was a knock at the door of Ganga Bhavajya's house. Thinking that her husband had returned, Devagiri Amma opened the door. But it was not her husband. An unknown old man entered the house. In this small village Devagiri Amma knew everyone. But this old man was unknown to her, and that too coming at such a late hour. She tried to find out who he was. The old man pleaded with her to allow him to remain inside the house for sometime as it was very cold outside. Being a pious lady Devagiri Amma asked the old man to sleep in the verandah, while she went inside her room, locking the door from inside. After sometime the old man knocked at her door. She opened the door. The old man said, "Mother, I am hungry. Please give me some food." She felt helpless since whatever food she had cooked had been eaten and nothing was left. She searched in the house for some eatables but found only a small quantity of flour. She mixed this flour with curds and served it to the old man who gratefully ate it. She then went into her room and prepared to go to sleep, locking the door from inside. Again after sometime there was a knock at her door. She opened the door only to again find the old man standing there. He told her that his legs were paining and requested her to massage them. She was perplexed at the way in which a complete stranger was behaving when her husband was not in the house. She wondered whether the old man was really a human being or whether Lord Shiva had come to test her. Without knowing what to do under such circumstances, she wept and prayed to Parvathi. She went out through the back door to procure the services of two or three servants for massaging the legs of the old man. She was willing to pay them liberally, but found none. She returned home disappointed and wondered what to do now, whether she ought to massage the legs of the old man or not. Who was this old man? She prayed to Parvati wholeheartedly to show her a way out of this predicament. The old man knocked at her door again. Just then a woman entered through the back door and addressed Devagiri Amma, "Mother, it seems you came to my house to engage me for massaging the legs of an old man. But at that time I was not in the house. Now I have come, please tell me to whom I should do the service?"

Devagiri Amma felt very happy. She presumed that on hearing her prayers Parvati must have sent this woman and she expressed her gratitude to the goddess. She sent the woman to the verandah to massage the legs of the old man while she went to her room and shut the door. After some time she opened the door again but she did not find either the old man or the woman sent to massage his legs. But in their place she saw Lord Shiva and Goddess Parvati. Her happiness knew no bounds and she felt at their feet. Then Parvati blessed her, "You shall have one son and one daughter." On hearing this, she again felt at the feet of Lord Shiva who blessed her, "Mother, I am pleased with your devotion, I will myself take birth as your third child." By the time she got up, both Lord Shiva and Goddess Parvati had disappeared.

She lay awake the whole night, waiting for her husband's return, to break the happy news of the visit of Lord Shiva and Parvati to their house. She saw only Lord

Shiva and Parvati, whether she closed or opened her eyes. At daybreak her husband returned home and she narrated everything to him. But he did not believe it. He told her sarcastically that she had gone mad or was dreaming. How could the gods come to their house? However much she tried to convince him about their visit he did not believe her.

In due course, Devagiri Amma gave birth to a male child and a female child a year after. As the children were born after so many years and that too blessed by Parvati Devi, Ganga Bhavajya started believing the visit of the gods to their house and the boons granted to his wife. From then onwards a lot of change came over him and he decided to do penance to have a vision and blessings of Lord Shiva and Goddess Parvati. He began to think that family attachments were obstacles for his penance.

While such ideas were taking concrete shape in him the third child started growing in the womb of Devagiri Amma. One day, Ganga Bhavajya took firm decision and informed his wife that he was retiring to the forests. As duty bound Devagiri Amma followed her husband. Without any money, placing complete faith in Lord Shiva and Parvati they proceeded towards an unknown destination in thick forests. On one hand Devagiri Amma felt elated that shortly Lord Shiva would be born to her. On the other hand she was worried and fearful of the aimless journey through forests. With these mixed feelings they continued their journey.

It was the 28th day of September, 1835. Ganga Bhavajya and Devagiri Amma were continuing their journey. The sun was rising, throwing light red-coloured rays on the earth. Devagiri Amma went into labour pains. She slowly reached a big banyan tree and lay down in its shade. Goddess Parvati was beside her unseen, giving her courage. All other gods were witnessing from above, this unique occasion of Lord Shiva being born in human form on the earth. This new 'Avatar' would put an end to religious fanaticism, jealousies, hatred, arrogance, egoism and attachments prevalent in the humans and would generate peace, *jnana,* love and equality among them. The gods showered flowers from above, unseen, and jubilant over the occasion. Great sages all over the world, for a moment became still and in that state witnessed the arrival of Lord Shiva in human form as Devagiri Amma's child. Finally Devagiri Amma delivered the child. No one knew that the new born Avatar of Lord Shiva would one day be known as Shirdi Sai Baba and that he would respond at once to the prayers of devotees, that he would show the way to a number of devotees for attaining salvation by becoming their Sadguru, and that even after his *Samadhi* he would protect his devotees.

Devagiri Amma was very happy that Lord Shiva himself was born to her. But Ganga Bhavajya was not satisfied by looking at the human child form of Lord Shiva. He was determined to see the real Lord Shiva and Goddess Parvati, as was seen by his wife. After sometime he prepared to set out on his journey. It was a testing moment for Devagiri Amma. On one side was her husband and she was duty bound to follow him. On another side, it is the just born child, apart from her weakness due to delivery. Finally, she decided to follow her husband, leaving the child in the forest. She prepared a small bed of leaves and spread a soft cloth over it. She placed her newborn child on the bed. She began weeping as other mothers do and the warm tears began to fall on the child. These tears were the last attachment between mother and child. She wept bitterly for not being in a position to provide food and shelter for her child. Perhaps, she was not aware that Adi Sankara, who can protect all the creations, does not require her protection.

No such thoughts were in Ganga Bhavajya. His aim was to have vision of Lord Shiva only. For achieving this family bonds and attachments would be hurdles. So he desired to be away from such attachments and go into the forest and do penance. He started to proceed towards his goal, his wife following him. For every step taken by her, the motherly love toward her newborn child began to melt into tears which flowed from her eyes continuously. She kept looking backwards at her child though advancing. The tears blocked her vision and she was able to see only a blurred image of her child. After proceeding for some more distance, she lost sight of her child completely and she followed her husband blindly. In the coming chapters we shall see where and how their aimless journey ended.

On the golden Kailash mountain, Lord Shiva should have been in the company at Parvati and other gods. But in his new 'Avatar' he was under the banyan tree, as a newborn child, moving his legs and hands playfully and waiting for the person who would find him and look after him. Lord Shiva knew who that person was. That Mahatma named Roshan Sha came in the form of a *fakir* (mendicant). When he was walking with his wife, he heard the cries of a small child. As they did not have any children, he picked up the child and gave him to his wife as a gift from 'Allah'.

We find no words to praise Roshan Sha and his wife who bathed Lord Shiva, and fed him. The child grew for four years till 1839 in the *fakir's* house. The actions of God cannot be gauged. How and when some persons come together and again get separated is beyond the understanding of common people. The *fakir* died one day. His wife brought up the child affectionately as her own.

In those days there were clashes between Hindus and Muslims. Under such conditions, the behaviour of this boy used to be peculiar. He would suddenly enter into a temple one day and start yelling, "Rama is God, Shiva is Allah". Both Hindus and Muslims used to admonish and punish him. On seeing this, Roshan Sha's wife used to suffer a lot. Finally, unable to withstand the complaints against the boy she decided to hand over the boy to a *sadhu* by name Venkusa in a nearby village.

"Om Shanti! Shanti! Shantihi"

CHAPTER 3

There was a village named Jambavavi, now in the State of Maharashtra, under the rule of a Nizam in those days. In this village there was a pious Brahmin named Keshava Rao and his wife. Both were devotees of Venkateswara at Lord Tirupathi. As they had no children, they always used to pray to the Lord to bless them with a child. One night the Lord appeared to Keshava Rao in a dream and told him that one Ramanand Yogi of Kashi would be born as their son shortly. After this Keshava Rao's wife became pregnant. He used to read the holy scriptures to his wife and explain them in detail. This was an exercise undertaken by him to impart *jnana* to the child who was in the womb of his wife. His wife gave birth to a male child on an auspicious day. The parents named him Gopal Rao, and imparted several types of education. When the boy reached marriageable age, they performed his marriage with a suitable girl.

Gopal Rao was a person of tact, strength, patience and knowledge. Above all this, he was a person with a helping nature and service. Pleased with his strength and courage, the Peshwas gave a paragana named Jintur as *jagir* to Gopal Rao to rule over this place. Gopal Rao loved the inhabitants of this place as his own children and ruled over them. He shifted his place of residence to the centrally located village Selu and developed it a lot. He inherited from his father, abundant devotion to Lord Venkateswara. Now and then the Lord would appear in his dreams. He established an ashram in his fort and gave opportunity to several people to lead saintly lives.

One evening, when he was taking a stroll in the fort, he found a young lady undressing for taking bath and Gopal Rao's mind had evil thoughts for a moment on seeing her naked form. Immediately regretting his perverted thoughts, he pierced both his eyes with a needle and lost his sight. Because of this, he could not discharge his duties as *jagirdar* properly. On the advise of his friends he performed special *puja* to Lord Venkateswara and regained his lost eyesight with the blessings of the Lord. From that day he came to be known as Venkudas (Lord Venkateswara's slave).

Roshan Sha's wife wanted to hand over the four-year-old boy to the care of Venkusa. But Venkusa was on a pilgrimage. He did not practise discrimination on account of religion, caste or creed. All were equal to him. He used to visit not only temples but also the *dargahs* and *gurudwaras* while on pilgrimage.

Once, when he visited the Sawaghahi Dargah in Ahmedabad, he heard the following words coming from there: "*Salaam alekum* Maharaj! You are born with a purpose. A hundred miles from Selu village there is another village by name Manwat. There Allah, who is born for setting this world right, is being brought up in a *fakir's* house. After you go back to Selu from your pilgirmage, the boy will be brought to you. You must accept this boy as your pupil and teach him. This is God's work. The boy will grow up in your care and will become 'Guru' for the entire world."

Venkusa returned to Selu after the pilgirmage. Roshan Sha's wife brought the boy and handed him over to Venkusa. Thus the boy (Baba) came under the care of Venkusa in his fifth year. Roshan Sha named the boy Majida and there are proofs that the boy grew under Venkusa with the name Majida.

Venkusa taught the boy all kinds of *shastras*. The boy who was born with natural Godliness learnt all of them in his early age. Venkusa took the boy along with him to other villages. In the year 1842 during summer, they both came to Shirdi village, and they stayed there for 7 days. They took their food in the house of Bayija Bai and slept in the small temples of the village. This means Baba came to Shirdi first in the year 1842. Perhaps, because of the food provided to him by Baija Bai, Baba used to call her Sister. Similarly, Baba in his young age came into contact with Nanavali.

Nanavali was younger than Baba. He used to do service at the *Samadhi* of a great person by name Nanavali, near Aurangabad. Hence he got the name of Nanavali and was known only by this name. During the tours of Venkusa along with Baba, they met Nanavali for the first time in 1849. Nanavali used to address Baba as Uncle. Having been brought up by Roshan Sha who was a Sufi saint, and later by Venkusa who was a devotee of Lord Venkateswara, Baba understood the important aspects of Islam and Hinduism and also the blind customs in both. Though Venkusa was a Hindu, he used to take Baba to the *Samadhis* of great persons of both the religions and explain their teachings and theories in detail.

Years rolled by. The boy who was born with a purpose, the incarnation of Lord Shiva, learnt everything related with physical, philosophical and other fields. He also learnt about "Pancha Bhutas" and the importance of the eight directions. He was able to feel the divine power which created this universe, and notice the unstable condition of life, soul, mind and arrogance. He also learnt the connection between these and the sensory organs and how to control desires and command the divine power in the body. A divine light in his eyes, sensibility in talk, calmness in his actions and mature thinking were found in him.

For Venkusa, his joy knew no bounds, for the boy whom he brought up acquired so many divine powers. He used to stare at the boy motionless, and tears would roll down from his eyes. Night and day he would keep the boy with him. He used to bathe him, dress him, feed him and put him to sleep. If sometimes he could not attend on the boy personally, he would suffer mentally. Whether it was natural love for the boy or whether it was the effect of the incarnation of Lord Shiva in the form of this boy, we do not know. Whatever it was, Venkusa's life was blessed since he acted as Baba's guru, protector, friend, mother and father. Though we do not know what Venkusa looked like, let us imagine and prostrate at his feet for having brought up our Sai, for having moulded him and presented him to crores of devotees throughout the world, let us prostrate at his feet for the second time. Sai is not merely a Guru. He is Samardha Sadguru. For having acted as Guru for such a Samardah Sadguru, let us prostate at the feet of Venkusa for the third time.

Since Venkusa brought up the boy with special care, the other ashramites, instead of showing love and affection towards the boy, developed jealous and hatred towards him. *Maya* appeared to be more powerful. Even though God himself had come to this world in human form, he could not escape from the clutches of *Maya.* In such case, what will be the fate of ordinary humans like us?

While Venkusa was teaching the boy the secrets in *shastras,* the other ashramites posed unnecessary and irrelevant questions which diverted the attention of Guru Venkusa. As he was not able to pay proper attention under such disturbed conditions, he took the boy into the forest and taught him in the different fields of education. The ashramites discovered the place where Venkusa was and sent a few disciples to bring him back to Selu. Suspecting that they were jealous of the boy and hated him, probably might harm him, without loss of time he inducted into the boy some of his powers on Suddha Dashami Day of the month of Asweeyuja. The boy who was just completing 16 years of age appeared fully mature, with divine powers.

Venkusa told the boy that he had done his duty as per God's decision and the day was not far off when they would be separated. He also told him that having achieved his goal, he would go into *Samadhi.* As per the *shastras* a disciple should not witness his guru attaining *Samadhi,* but if he went back to Selu or the neighbouring villages, the people there might harm him. If they continued to be together then also the people who were jealous of them would be haunting them. Therefore, it was necessary that they be separated. On a full-moon day, Venkusa inducted into the boy all his remaining powers. It was decided that Venkusa would return to Selu and the boy would proceed along the shores of Godavari river. The plan was found out by some spies from Selu and the news was carried over to Selu. From Selu Venkusa's successors secretly came to the forest and watched their movements.

The people of Selu, thinking that Venkusa had left his family, ashram and properties for the sake of this boy, planned to kidnap the boy so that Venkusa would return to Selu. Sensing such a move, Venkusa protected the boy by staying with him every moment. Since the village people found that it was very difficult to kidnap the boy, they decided to kill him. That night was *Chaturdasi,* a day prior to full moon. The conspirators were discussing the methods of killing the boy. They had not bring knives or sticks with them. There were no big stones nearby. While this was the situation, Venkusa and the boy prepared to go to sleep.

The boy had peaceful sleep, whereas Venkusa could not sleep as he was preoccupied with thoughts of the boy. One of the conspirators, with a view not to delay their plan further, took a brick which was lying nearby and wanting to kill the boy at one stroke, proceeded towards him. Venkusa, who was half asleep, suddenly opened his eyes and found the brick coming towards the boy's head. He at once put his own head in the path of the brick which hit his forehead and caused bleeding. With blazing eyes Venkusa cursed him, who fell dead the next moment. Hearing the commotion the boy woke up from his sleep and observed everything. The other two conspirators who were at a distance ran away, lest they also die by the curse of Venkusa.

The boy tore off a piece of cloth from his dress and cleaned the injury suffered by Venkusa. They were staring at each other with different thoughts in their minds. While Venkusa was thinking that even at the risk of losing his life, he would hand over the boy as Guru to posterity, the boy was thinking how to repay the debt to his Guru for having protected him. Thus the hearts of Guru and disciple became one, ideas became one, with love and affection in harmony. Such should be the binding force between Guru and disciple.

The sun began to rise in the east with the red rays spreading over the sky. Venkusa and the boy both took their bath in the river. Venkusa milked a nearby cow and pouring the milk into the hands of the boy, imparted all the remaining powers he had and commanded the boy to bring to life one of the conspirators who lay dead due to the curse given by Venkusa. The boy washed the toe of the right foot of the Guru and sprinkled this water on the dead person who came alive, saying he regreted his attempt to kill the boy and sought his pardon.

Venkusa wanted to give the boy all the valuable ornaments he was wearing but the boy declined to have them. Instead he requested Venkusa to give him the brick which had hit him on his forehead while saving him (boy) from the murderous attack. Overwhelmed by his request and with tears rolling down from his eyes, Venkusa gave him the brick with his blessings. He wished that the brick always be the boy's companion and life partner. The boy also requested Guru Venkusa to give him the piece of cloth drenched with blood while cleaning his injury. Moved emotionally by such a request Venkusa tied the cloth piece around the forehead of the boy and declared that it would protect the boy at all times. He told him to proceed along the banks of river Godavari and the place where he found complete peace would be abode. He also advised him to keep away from women and wealth. Afterwards Venkusa proceeded to Selu along with the revived person.

After walking for three days along the banks of River Godavari, the boy reached a place called Kopargaon in the year 1854, *Margashira* month on the third day after full moon. After taking rest for a day he again proceeded and reached the village of Shirdi by evening. Not willing to approach anyone for shelter, he began to live under the shade of a big neem tree.

Om Shanti! Shanti! Shantihi!

CHAPTER 4

After giving birth to the child Avatar on 28 September, 1835, Devagiri Amma and Ganga Bhavajya continued their journey aimlessly in the forests. Though he went with detachment, he observed the physical weakness and helplessness in his wife Devagiri Amma. Sympathy evoked in him, but he thought that he should not succumb to such weakness, and so started proceeding further. But Devagiri Amma was too weak to walk straight and her sight was getting blurred, her tongue drying up with thirst. She had no physical strength at all. But as a devout woman, she followed her husband slowly. With great difficulty they moved ahead. Ganga Bhavajya stopped near a freshwater tank. He could not proceed further after seeing the condition of his wife. He tried to suppress his feelings unsuccessfully. All his feelings and sympathies for his wife gushed out and he thought Lord Shiva would not give him *Darshan* if he left his wife alone and proceeded. He went to her and started attending on her. After quenching her thirst she went into deep sleep, fully exhausted. In the meantime a *banjara* (a nomad) who was passing by saw them and told them that if they did not leave that place before dusk, there was danger from wild animals. So saying he took them along with him for some distance and showed them a hut. He told them that this hut belonged to him and they could rest in it. After sometime the *banjara's* wife brought food for them and after serving them they all sat together. The *banjara* couple heard the story of their guests attentively. Then they addressed the guests.

"The norms for leading an ordinary type of life are prescribed in the *Vedas.* They are of four kinds, viz., *Dharma, Artha, Kama* and *Moksha.* Every man should follow these four during his lifetime. The woman, while being the life companion, should assist the man in attaining them. This is the speciality in Hindu culture. But having brought forth three children, you left them mercilessly and took to the forests. Your action goes against the *dharma.* It is good to desire a vision of Lord Shiva. If that is life's aim, one should be a *sanyasi* and not *grihastha* (family man). But being *grihastha,* forgetting one's duties towards family, one should not seek God, for this is not correct. After performing all your duties only you should take to *vanaprastha* (retiring to the forests) and then seek God. This is *Dharma Marga.* As you have already abondoned your three children you should now proceed. Though you are wife and husband, in future you should not have any bodily attachments, but concentrate on doing penance for *Atma Sakshatkara* and then for the *Sakshatkara* of Lord Shiva . There is a village named Nivasa about 150 miles from here and from there you proceed another 20 miles and do your penance."

The words of the *banjara* was like the chanting of the *Vedas* and Ganga Bhavajya decided to do penance with his wife for the *Sakshatkara* of Lord Shiva. In the meantime, the *banjara* gave them two wild fruits from the forest and made them eat, by which they got rid of all bodily ailments, attaining divine powers necessary for doing penance. Late in the night they slept. When Ganga Bhavajya woke up in the morning, he found neither the *banjara* couple nor the hut. All that had taken place the previous night appeared to them as a dream.

Devagiri Amma regained her physical health and was happy. After travelling for eleven days, they reached the place on the banks of Godavari river, as indicated by the *banjara,* and started their penance for years. Many used to visit them and learn spiritual matters from them. The devotees named Devagiri Amma as Dwarakamai. Devagiri means Govardhanagiri, the mountain lifted by Lord Krishna and the place surrounding it is Dwaraka, and *Aai* means mother. Similarly, Ganga Bhavajya was named Gurudhan because he was imparting *jnana* to the seekers. So, the names acquired by the parents of Baba, in the *Jnana Marga,* were Gurudhan and Dwarakamai. As many people started visiting them, it caused disturbance for their penance, and so they shifted into the interior forest. Both used to be in a state of *Samadhi* for days together.

After reaching Shirdi, Baba lived for sometime under a neem tree on the outskirts of the village. Some villagers with their unnecessary talk, were disturbing Baba's meditation. For a long time he used to go into the nearby forest and remain there all the day, eating fruits and other things available in the forest. After a certain period, some of the villagers noticed this boy who used to sit under the neem tree under all extreme climatic conditions, and always meditating. Some of them asked the same question direct to the boy, thereby disturbing his meditation. While this was so, some people who were carefully observing him recognised him as a boy with unusual divine powers. But many used to talk about him critically and used to poke fun at him.

One day a blind person came and sat in the shade of the neem tree. Some rowdies abused him and threw him aside and went away. This commotion disturbed the meditation of the boy. He found out the reason for the commotion. Feeling pity for the blind person, the boy with his divine hands, cleaned both the eyes and catching the eyelids firmly with his hands passed his divine rays from his eyes into those of the blind man. Unable to bear the agony of burning eyes, the blind man cried aloud and fainted. The rowdies who had ill-treated the blind man earlier assembled there with some others. After a short time, the blind man regained his consciousness and found that he was no longer blind. Seeing this, the people assembled there were wonderstruck. From then onwards not only the villagers of Shirdi but also those from neighbouring villages started coming to the boy for getting their ailments cured. Thus, a year passed.

Sometimes, the boy used to take the juice of any leaf found nearby and gave it as medicine. Whatever seed he found he used to ask the patient to make a paste of it and use it as medicine. If he touched the ailing limb of the body the ailment would disappear. Slowly, people recognised him as a great physician. The entire day time he used to treat the patients. In the nights some persons used to come and disturb him with unnecessary questions. As he was not able to meditate properly due to the conditions prevailing, one night he left Shirdi and proceeded eastwards along the bank of River Godavari. He reached Triambakeswar and finding the high mountains suitable for his meditation, he started doing penance.

The brick given to him by Guru Venkusa was his only companion, and the piece of cloth soaked with the blood of his Guru was his protector. He did penance for a year. Afterwards he returned by the same route along the banks of River Godavari via Kopargaon and reached the place where he and his Guru Venkusa had parted on exactly on the same day of the same month. As two years had lapsed since then, he found that many trees had come up around the place like a thick forest. He found it difficult to exactly pinpoint the place. Then he took out the brick and tied it in the blood-soaked piece of cloth and prayed to his Guru. Immediately, the entire area became as it was two years back. Instantly, he recognised the spot where his Guru had saved him from an attack to kill him. He prayed: "Oh Guruji! You shed your blood to save me! I want to have your *Darshan*." Then he heard the voice of his Guru telling him. "I attained *Samadhi* in Selu. I cannot come out of the *Samadhi* and give you *darshan*. But my power will always be protecting you." Then the boy said, "I do not have parents, borthers or other relatives. You are the only person for me. I must have your *darshan* today as you have saved my life. Otherwise, I do not want to live further. I will take out my life by hitting myself with the same brick from which you saved me two years back." So saying he hit his forehead with the brick. Suddenly, the hand of his Guru Venkusa appeared in between the brick and his forehead. Venkusa stood next to him and blessed him. He told the boy: "Because of your faith and gratitude towards me I had to get up from my *Samadhi* and come to you. I appreciate your devotion for your Guru. You will become Guru for the entire world. Like me you will also bless your devotees from your *Samadhi.* I am giving this boon to you. You have descended from Lord Shiva. The boon I give you now is only symbolic. Even after you attain *Samadhi* you will be saving your devotees from the *Maya* of Kali. This is possible only for Lord Shiva who drank poison and kept it in his throat. As I have come out of *Samadhi,* I will be with you for two years in an invisible form. Continue your penance." So saying Guru Venkusa disappeared. The boy remained in the same place for two years doing penance. Whenever necessary, Guru Venkusa used to advise him in the invisible form. In the year 1858, again on a full-moon day in the month of *Margashira,* he gave him *darshan* and told him to go back to Shirdi. He further told him that he would also be there in the form of a *jyoti* (burning light) near the neem tree in an underground structure.

The penance undertaken by Gurudhan (Ganga Bhavajya) and Dwarakamai (Devagiri Amma) reached the climax stage. Pleased with their penance Shiva and Parvati appeared before them. Overjoyed at the *Sakshatkar,* they pleaded with Lord Shiva and Goddess Parvati to give them *moksha* (salvation). Agreeing to this, Lord Shiva told them, "You will get *moksha* as desired by you. But you two, in the form of *jyotis* (burning lights) will remain permanently in the underground structure near the neem tree at Shirdi. Another Mahatma by name Venkusa will also be there with you as *jyoti.* Gurudhan will remain there permanently. In the coming days, I will keep Dwarakamai in a nearby place in the form of *Dhuni.* Similarly I shall arrange a suitable place for Venkusa. After my present 'Avatar' comes to an end, I will get the physical remains of my body placed in between you two. In this way, Shirdi will be the abode of four divine powers and for the coming 500 years it will grow day by day and will be Kailash for the devotees." So saying Lord Shiva put his hand *(Abhaya Hastha)* towards them. Immediately, two dazzling light rays emerged from the hand and entered the bodies of Gurudhan and Dwarakamai, bringing out their inner life *(prana shakti)* in the form of *jyotis* and coming out from their upper skull. In an invisible form these *jyotis* reached Shirdi village and under the neem tree in an underground structure remained there doing penance. Similarly Venkusa came out from his *Samadhi* at Selu and came to Shirdi in the form of *jyoti* and joined the other two in the underground structure near the neem tree.

There the boy (Baba), after having *darshan* of Venkusa, proceeded till he reached a village called Dhoop near Aurangabad by sunset and took rest near a big boulder. At the same time the Patel *(munsif)* of Dhoop village, Chand Bai, having lost his horse, started searching for it with the saddle on his shoulder. Having roamed for the horse, he became tired and wanted to relax and so came to the place where the boy (Baba) was taking rest.

Noticing Chand Bai, Baba questioned him, "What Chand Bai! You seem to be tired after searching for your horse." Chand Bai was surprised at how this stranger knew his name and about the missing horse. The boy replied that he knew everything and there was nothing he did not know. Then Chand Bai asked the boy to tell him where to find his lost horse named Bijli. The boy asked Chand Bai to proceed on the right side for some distance and there would be a small pond where he could find his horse Bijli grazing. Chand Bai said that he had come from that side and had not found his horse there and there was no use going there again. To this the boy replied that his words would not go in vain and one should have complete faith to have result. No one can get the result with a doubtful mind. He asked him to go and get the horse. But this appeared unbelievable truth for Chand Bai. While they were discussing thus, the boy took out a smoking pipe and tobacco from his bag. To use the pipe for smoking, water was required and to light the tobacco, fire was required. The boy, with his metal rod-like instrument *(sataka)* struck the ground before him. Immediately water came out in the form of a jet. After preparing the pipe by filling it with tobacco he struck for the second time at the same place on the ground with his *sataka* and fire came out this time. The boy then lighted the tobacco with this fire. He smoked from the pipe and passed it to Chand Bai for smoking. Dumbstruck by these acts of the boy, Chand Bai wondered whether what he was seeing was real or only a dream. After realising that this was not a dream, Chand Bai ran towards the direction given by the boy earlier and found his horse 'Bijli' grazing near the pond. He came back with the horse and prostated before the boy. He invited him to come along with him to his house. With great devotion he made the boy sit on the horse and he walked along beside the horse.

If the boy with such divine powers step into his house, all the evils haunting would go away and peace and happiness would come to the place. So thought Chand Bai. The boy remained as guest of Chand Bai for 35 days, blessing the people of Dhoop village. Afterwards, on a request from Chand Bai, the boy accompanied the marriage party of Chand Bai's brother-in-law and came in a bullock cart to Shirdi, which was the bride's place. Chand Bai thought that if they took this boy with the divine powers along with them there would not be any obstacles and the marriage celebrations would go on peacefully.

The bullock carts of the marriage party were proceeding towards Shirdi. In the evening cool winds started blowing and the bells tied round the necks of the bullocks were giving rhythmic sounds mingled with the singing of the birds. At dusk the red rays from the setting sun from the west began to fall on the white clouds in the east and the scene was pleasing to the eyes. As if welcoming the Mahatma (Baba) sitting in front in the bullock cart, the birds started chirping and flying before the cart. From a distance the *koel* (nightingale) was singing as if saying: "God is coming to Shirdi personally to settle down there. Do not think under the influence of *Maya* that he is only an ordinary person. So you all please recognise him as God." The moon appeared on the east as if to give light to the Mahatma. The entire marriage party was full of joy and enjoying peace every moment. Thus the marriage party proceeded towards Shirdi.

The entire nature was blooming to welcome this God incarnation from Kailash. Those of the marriage party who witnessed this were really lucky. Similarly, with a prayer that we should also get an opportunity to be with Baba at least for a few months either in this birth or in future births, we end this chapter.

Om Shanti! Shanti! Shantihi!

First Day's 'Parayana' is over

SECOND DAY'S PARAYAN — FRIDAY

CHAPTER 5

Without experiencing any kind of difficulties the marriage party reached Shirdi safely. None of them felt tired or exhausted. Chand Bai Patil believed that because they had the *fakir* in the first cart, their journey was without any obstacles and ended happily. The bullock carts stopped by a big banyan grove by the side of Khandoba temple. The members of the marriage party alighted there and went to the houses provided for them by the bride's parents. But the young *fakir* got down slowly from the cart after all others left, and started walking with divine light. On seeing the young *fakir,* Mhalsapathi recognised him as God incarnation. He used to mostly read the poems *(dohe)* of Kabir. In his poems Kabir used to address God as 'Sai'. Mhalsapathi, who was the 'Pujari' of 'Khandoba' temple, on seeing the young *fakir,* came out of the temple and with folded hands addressed him as "Welcome Sai". In this way the *fakir* got the name as 'Sai' from Mahalsapathi. Afterwards he became famous as "Sai Baba". Baba means father.

Baba went to the neem tree where he used to sit and meditate on previous occasions. The divine powers of Gurudhan, Dwarakamai and Venkusa which were in the underground structure in the form of *jyotis,* conversed with him. Ordinary persons could not see or hear them. In this way Sai Baba reached Shirdi for the second time, in the year 1858. For nearly two years he used to beg for food from five houses daily and he lived under the neem tree. During daytime he used to go to the nearby forest and remain alone. Sometimes he used to remain in the forest for four or five days without food or water. There were two other saintly persons at Shirdi, named Devidas and Janakidas. They recognised Baba as a person with extraordinary divine powers and used to converse with him frequently. Mhalsapathi also used to visit Baba under the neem tree, now and then. Some people of Shirdi recognised Baba as the same person who had sat under this neem tree a few years back and cured the villagers of their ailments. So they started visiting Baba again for getting their ailments cured. Baba soon got the name of a doctor or *vaidya,* with extraordinary divine powers. They shifted the residence of Baba from the neem tree to a dilapidated mosque nearby, which they repaired making it fit for residence. Sometime in the year 1860, Baba used to visit the following five houses daily, begging for food: (1) Ganapathi Rao's son Tatya Patil (2) Vaman Sakharam (3) Nandu Savai Rama Vani (4) Madhava Rao Deshpande (Shama) and (5) Appaji Patil.

There was an elementary school adjoining the mosque. Shama was working there as teacher. He used to be nearer to Sai Baba. Mhalsapathi also used to visit Sai frequently and used to spend time with him till late in the nights, discussing several matters. Shama also used to join their discussions. Ganapathi Rao's wife Baija Bai and his son Tatya developed immense love and respect for Sai Baba. They used to take their food only after Sai had visited their house and taken alms. But the village *munsif* "Bhate" had a different opinion about Sai. He used to talk evil of Sai, saying that he was a cheat and wasting others' time by his lectures.

In the year 1861, during the rainy season there was a severe cyclone. The small hut in which a leper named Bhagoji Shinde lived was swept away by the cyclone. A shivering Bhagoji approached some known persons for shelter, but none gave him shelter in their house fearing that they may contact leprosy. Not knowing what to do, he proceeded towards the mosque where Sai was, with the hope that Sai would come to his rescue. But on the way, due to severe cold and rain he fell down crying "Sai". Sai immediately ran towards him, lifted him and carried him on his shoulders to the mosque. A fire was required immediately to keep Bhagoji warm. But no fire could be lit in that severe cyclone. So Baba called Mother Dwarakamai who was in the underground structure near the neem tree, in the form of a *jyoti.* Immediatly Dwarakamai, in an invisible form, came and lighted the firewood in the mosque. Bhagoji regained consciousness after getting warmth from the fire in the mosque. Bhagoji's leprosy disappeared completely after Sai Baba touched his body, followed by the warmth given by Dwarakamai.

Within minutes the news about Bhagoji's cure of his leprosy spread in the village. The villagers of Shirdi who recognised 'Sai' till then as a doctor and a great person, started to worship him as God. From that day Baba named the mosque as Dwarakamai. Gurudhan and Venkusa were there in the underground structure near the neem tree in the form of *jyotis.* Hence, Sai Baba named that place as Gurusthan. From that day the fire which was started in Dwarakamai (mosque) continues to burn and is called Dhuni. The ash (*vibhuti* or *udi*) from the Dhuni had the power to cure ailments and Sai Baba used to give it to the patients instead of medicines.

One day, Nanavali came to Shirdi, and because of his old acquaintance with Baba, addressed him as Uncle. *(Mama, Kaka).* Baba asked him to keep quiet, saying there was no place for old acquintances or connections, the only connection being spiritual. Nanavali understood Baba's advice well and lived separately in Shirdi. He used to love Baba more than his life, and if anyone talked ill of Baba, he used to condemn them. Though he was younger in age to Baba, he was an *Avadhuta.*

Slowly all the villagers of Shirdi started coming closer to Baba. They used to start any work only after informing Baba. Though Baba was an adult he used to play with the children sometimes. Sometimes he used to roam about in the forest. Baija Bai used to bring food for Baba daily and only after Baba ate, she took her food. Sometimes when Baba went into the forest, she used to go in search of him and only after giving him food, would she return to her house and take her food. Her son Tatya used to accompany her. He used to play on the shoulders of Baba, calling him Uncle.

Shirdi village became famous because of Sai Baba. He was highly intellectual and good-natured. He had no love for material things, but was always thinking of *Atma.* His heart was as clear as a mirror. He never bowed to desires. He never differentiated between the rich and the poor. Though he was living at Shirdi he knew what was happening at distant places. Though he had all the powers *(siddhis)* at his feet, he never used them.

The mere touch of Sai's feet will detach us from worldly attachments and help us in getting *Atma Sakshatkara* (self-realisation). His *Pada Tirth* (water with which his feet are washed) has the power of destroying the evil forces. His *udi (vibhuti)* will cure all types of ailments. His order or command is like one from the *Vedas.* He never appeared tired. He never exhibited displeasure or overjoy. He was always in a happy mood. Everyone realised this true state of Sai Baba soon.

In the earlier days, Gowli Buva, who was a staunch devotee of Vittal, had expressed about Sai Baba as follows: "Baba has come into this world for the sake of orphans and the downtrodden." At one time Baba had a bout of wrestling with Mohiuddin Tamboli and pretended to lose. But from that day the egoism in Mohiuddin was removed and he stopped wrestling bouts, slowly working towards self-realisation *(Atma Sakshatkara).* A false Guru named Jowahar Ali from Ahmadnagar came to Shirdi and told everyone that Sai Baba was his pupil *(shishya)* and took him along with him to Rahata, a nearby village. Without any protest Baba followed Jowhar Ali and served him as his pupil for about six months. Even though several defects were found in the false Guru, Baba, without complaining, served him sincerely, thus showing to the world how a pupil should behave towards his Guru. Afterwards, the villagers of Shirdi exposed the false Guru and brought Baba back to Shirdi.

After experiencing Baba's love towards them while he was at Shirdi, and missing it while he was away at Rahata, the villagers realised the greatness of him. They realised that Sai Baba was just like a mother to them and his words were full of nectar. Some devotees shed tears out of joy at Baba's return to Shirdi from Rahata. Sai Baba gave them the following message:

"You should never think I am nearer to you or at a distant place. I will be knowing from any distance your actions. I am the ruler of your hearts. I am in every atom of all matter and living beings in this world. I am the Creator, Preserver and Destroyer of this world. Whoever concentrates his thoughts on me will have nothing to fear. But *Maya* will punish those who forget me."

On hearing authentically about Sai Baba's true state and his words which were like nectar, the devotees prostrated before him. Irrespective of age and sex, they started visiting him before attending to their other works. Baba give *udi* as *prasad* to all the devotees who visited him. Baba, with his huge personality used to wear a long shirt *(kafni)* from top to bottom and tie the piece of cloth given to him by his Guru Venkusa, around his head. He used to carry a big bag *(jholi)* on his left shoulder. He rarely changed his clothes. Sometimes he used to give the clothes for washing, whenever his devotees insisted. He used to give some of the food he got from the five houses, to the domestic animals and birds, some he used to put in the Dhuni for his mother and used to eat only the remaining. Sometimes the animals and birds used to put their mouths and beaks inside the pot in which the food was put, but Baba never objected.

Sometimes Baba used to tie small bells around his legs and sing divine songs and dance near a place called Takiya. His voice was very pleasing. Sometimes, when he sang with full fervour, not only the devotees but also the animals used to watch him and enjoy his music.

In those days there used to be Hindu-Muslim religious differences in most parts of the country. The English who ruled the country, wantonly used to create such differences. In view of the then prevailing conditions Baba never disclosed anything about his parents or the details of his birth. He dressed like a Muslim *fakir.* He used to have firewood continuosly burning in the Dhuni (a Hindu custom) in the mosque. He grew a *tulasi* (basil) plant in the left front side of the mosque. In this way he used to follow both Hindu and Muslim customs. He thus drew devotees from both the religions and used to teach them religious tolerance and co-existence.

In due course Sai Baba's name reached far-off places like Bombay. Ailments which could not be cured with medicines, got cured with the *udi* given by Sai Baba. His *pada tirtha* acted like *sanjeevani* (the herb that cured Lakshmana in the war with Ravana). Problems which could not be solved earlier got solved, before the devotees reached their respective places after praying to Baba personally. Not only Hindus and Muslims but also Sikhs, Parsis and Christians came to Sai.

Mhalsapati used to perform *Puja* to Baba personally every day. Shama used to look after the needs of devotees. Baba used to ask some devotees for *dakshina* (alms). He declined it from some devotees who voluntarily offered. He used to distribute the amount collected by way of *dakshina* to poor people who depended on him.

The village *munsif* Bhate did not like what Baba was doing, thinking that he was practising black magic and mesmerism. Bhate tried to find some drawbacks or defects in Baba so that he could be proved to be a cheat in the eyes of his devotees.

Sai Baba liked lighting the lamps very much. He used to request the village oil merchants to donate oil which with he used to light the lamps in the mosque. Bhate persuaded the oil merchants not to donate oil to Baba, for then Baba would not be able to light the lamps in the mosque and everyone would come to know of his incapacity.

Sai Baba, without worrying over it, asked Bhagoji to bring some water. He drank the water and later vomitted it in a vessel. This water turned into oil with which Bhagoji lighted the lamps and they burned the whole night. The oil merchants, who had declined to donate oil, and were watching this, seeing the lights burning with water, ran up to Baba and fell at his feet, pleading for forgiveness.

Devotees out of love for Baba used to do *pada puja* (offer prayers at his feet) daily. They also put sandalpaste on the hands and gave *arathi* with camphor. Though Baba had no desire for all this, he never objected to their actions. A Muslim devotee of Baba, Rohilla, out of religious fanaticism, wanted to kill Baba, because he was allowing ringing of bells, giving *arathi,* etc., in the mosque which went against Islamic doctrine. So, one night he waited for an opportune time to hit Baba with a big stick. When Baba came out of the mosque for a stroll, Rohilla tried to hit him. Immediately Baba turned around and with his eyes wide open focussed them on Rohilla. Two light rays came out of Baba's eyes and fell on the hands of Rohilla. Immediately, the stick dropped to the ground from his hands. Baba lifted his own hands and showed Rohilla his palms. Rohilla saw Mecca Medina and the sacred *Quran* in the palms of Sai Baba. Saying "Ya Allah", he fell at the feet of Baba.

Sai Baba tried his best to establish friendship between the Hindus and the Muslims. The gist of Baba's teachings are as follows: "Rama who is worshipped by the Hindus and Rahim by the Muslims, are one and the same. There is no difference between them. When it is so, why do the respective devotees quarrel among themselves? All religions and communties should become united as brothers, and work towards national integration. No benefits come from disputes, clashes, etc. Do not compete with others. You take care of your own advancement. *Yoga, thyaga, tapas* and *jnana* are the four ways for attaining *moksha.* One can choose one out of the four to attain *moksha.* Do not harm anyone because he has harmed you. Whatever good is possible you go on doing for others."

Sai Baba never exhibited his superiority. He did not have any attachment for his body. He had endless love for his devotees. He used to tell the past, present and future of his devotees! Friends and foes were equal for him. Though the villagers of Shirdi did not have the required *jnana,* they had endless love and devotion for him.

Baba had all the six natural qualities found in God. They are fame, wealth, detachment, *jnana,* super power and magnanimity.

The assurances given by Baba to the devotees are follows: "I am slave among slaves. I am indebted to you. I am contented with your *darshan.* I am gratified with your *pada darshan.* I am like a worm in your excretion." From these words of Baba one can decide how much love and affection he had for his devotees.

Though he appeared in the human form, he is God Incarnation. He resided in the hearts of all. He never had any attachment for anything or anyone in his heart. But outwardly, he appeared like a man of many desires. He was always peaceful. But sometimes he used to abuse and talk aloud like a mentally deranged person. Always he used to think about *Atma.* He used to say "Allah Malik". He used to lean against the wall of the mosque and distribute *udi* as *prasad* to devotees.

In the beginning, Mhalsapathi also thought that Baba was a Muslim *fakir.* But as the acquaintance with him grew, and when Baba lighted the lamps with water, then he believed that he was God Incarnated and worshipped him in the same manner as he worshipped God. He used to give *arathi.* Immersed in devotion, he used to sing devotional songs. This was the daily routine of Mhalsapathi. Muslim devotees like Rohilla and Rangari adjusted themselves to the ways Baba was worshipped by the Hindus. But some Muslim fanatics, acting on the advice of their religious leader of Sangamner, gathered about ten strong men with sticks and surrounded Baba's mosque. They warned that anyone who tried to enter the mosque to worship Baba in the Hindu way, would be beaten to death. Mhalsapathi, who was very timid by nature, worshipped Baba from a distance.

Having noticed the situation Baba called Mhalsapathi and asked him to come inside the mosque and do *puja* as usual: "I will see who will harm you," So saying Baba struck the floor with his *sataka.* On hearing Baba's roaring voice, all the Muslims who were near the mosque carrying sticks, ran away in fear. But Mhalsapathi could not get over the fear that gripped him. He began to fear that they might harm him on his way home and told Baba about his fear. Then Baba, pitying him, gave him the following assurance. "Either these persons or any other person, here or elsewhere, either in your present birth or future births, cannot do any harm to you. I will be guarding you with a thousand eyes. I will continue to protect you. You can go home without any fear." Such assurances have not been given by any other god till now.

May the assurance given to Mhalsapathi by Baba apply even now to those devotees who read this *Life History of Sai Baba.* Let foes become friends. Let the devotees have peace and happiness in the name of Sai.

Om Shanti ! Shanti ! Shantihi !

CHAPTER 6

After starting Dhuni in Dwarakamai, Baba used to sit leaning on the wall opposite the Dhuni, most of the day. Thus sitting in front of his mother who gave him this physical body, he would tell about his feelings to her. He frequently used to say "Masjid Mai" which meant mosque mother. Now and then he used to convey his feeling to the mother.

As long as the physical body is there, attachments will be there. Once the life leaves the body, then there are no such attachments. For sages, saints and those who want to free themselves from this lifecycle, this state gives them peace and happiness to their soul. But ordinary people, after their death, seek rebirth as they are not able to come out of their worldly desires. If you do not have such desires, then there will not be a rebirth or *punar janma.* This is *moksha* or *mukthi* or *salvation.*

With great detachment, having got *moksha,* Gurudhan, Dwarakamai and Venkusa in the form of *jyotis* were in Shirdi only for the welfare and prosperity of the masses and not for the sake of themselves. Under such a state, there would not be any relationship as mother and son. All were equal and in such a state only, all were at Shirdi. Sai was visible in the human form whereas the other three were not—this was the only difference.

After devotees like Mhalsapathi and others worshipped Baba in the morning, he used to sit opposite the Dhuni and do some soul-searching. At about noon, he went into the village for alms. He put solid foods like *roti* in his bag and the liquid in a small vessel. If his visit was not noticed by someone, he would softly call out "*Fakir* has come mother". If some looked into his eyes at the time of giving alms, they used to get full happiness and they desired to have any number of re-births just to look at the eyes of Baba. Such things were experienced only by devotees who realised Sai's divinity. Persons like Bhate, the village *munsif,* who never came near Sai or spoke to him used to criticise and abuse him. But Baba, for whom bouquets and brickbats were the same, ignored such things. He used to take rest in the afternoons. In the evenings, he grew flower plants in the backyard of the mosque and also in the vacant land called Lendi Bagh on the west side of Gurusthan. Tatya, who was a small boy when Baba came to Shirdi, who used do sit on the lap of Baba and played, had now grown up and spent most of his time with Baba. Baba was more precious to him than his own life. They should have been together in the previous births also. Tatya attended to all the needs of Baba. He kept the mosque clean and attended to its repairs, bringing firewood for the Dhuni, changing the dress of Baba and watering the flower plants in Lendi Bagh. Mhalsapathi similarly had come close to Baba.

Now and then Baba used to feed the poor with the amount that he received by way of *dakshina.* On such occasions he went personally to the market and purchased all the required material. Tatya would assist Baba in bringing them to the mosque, in cooking and serving the food. Baba used to personally check to see whether the salt etc., were put in the correct proportions in the food. Sometimes Baba cooked and served non-vegetarian food. He put his hand in the vessel to stir the boiling food. But nothing happened to his hand even then.

One day Baba personally cooked food and fed the poor. The food had to be cooked two or three times as hundreds of poor people attended and this went on till sunset. That day for some reason or the other, Tatya did not come to the mosque in the daytime. Baba had to attend to the entire work all alone. Tatya came in the evening and learnt about the feeding of the poor and how Baba had to attend to the work all alone. He regretted very much for not having assisted Baba. He found Baba completely exhausted which worried him. Meanwhile, Mhalsapathi came there. Tatya told him about the condition of Baba and sought his advise as to how to make Baba take rest. In spite of tiredness Baba went near the Dhuni and sat there. Mhalsapathi told Tatya that if they could bring a nice big stone and put it outside the mosque, then Baba could take complete rest sitting on the stone in the moonlight and enjoy the cool breeze.

All of them finished taking their night meal and everything was silent. Late in the night Tatya told Mhalsapathi that he would go to the nearby mountainside and bring a big stone for Baba. But Baba who was hearing their conversation, asked Tatya not to go. But Tatya would not listen, blamed himself for Baba's exhaustion and as a punishment he was determined to go and get the stone. Mhalsapathi also pleaded with Tatya not to go during the night, but he was stubborn.

Baba told Tatya that a big stone for him to sit in the open yard would come and he need not go to bring it. But Tatya insisted on getting it immediately, saying that he would not have satisfaction if somebody else brought the stone and hence he himself would bring it. So saying he went out of the mosque. As Baba did not want to give trouble at such an odd hour in the night, he lifted his two hands and made some gestures and talked something to himself. Suddenly, there was a big lightning. Tatya and Mhalsapathi, unable to withstand the lightning closed their eyes. On opening their eyes, they found a big flat stone with red and white colours, in front of the mosque. Both were surprised at this. Baba in the moonlight sat on the stone with one leg over the other. Lifting his right hand he showed them his *Abhaya Hastha*. Mhalsapathi saw Lord Shiva in Baba, while Tatya saw Maruthi in Baba. Thus Baba appeared to them in two forms simultaneously. Out of joy Mhalsapathi's eyes brimmed with tears and he recited some *shlokas* on Shiva. When they came back to their original state, Baba made them sit down and personally served them meals.

He cautioned them not to reveal to anyone what they had seen of the *leelas* of Baba. He always concentrated on his Guru and got maximum satisfaction loving him. Thus he had the complete blessings of his Guru. He merged himself with him. When one gets into such a state, one can see in one's Guru, Guru Brahma, Guru Vishnu, Gurudevo Maheshwarah, Guru Sakshat Parabrahma. But if one simply utters "Guruji" without following his teachings, then the word 'Guru' will remain only a word used to give respect to the Guru. But such a pupil cannot obtain any benefit from his Guru.

Because of Baba's state of concentration, all *siddhis* and *aishwaryas* (prosperities) came to his feet. These *siddhis* were capable of misguiding even *yogis* and destroying them. Hence, Baba discouraged them. He did not even look at them. All those powerful *siddhis* were lying at Baba's feet for nearly 30 years. He did not exhibit his extraordinary powers till 1886.

I pray that readers be blessed with devotion, *jnana* and detachment and that those who read this chapter with devotion be endowed with concentration of their minds.

Om Shanti ! Shanti ! Shantihi !

CHAPTER 7

The time-wheel was moving fast. Along with it Sai Baba's name had spread to all places in Maharashtra. Devotees from different places visited Sai Baba and got solutions to their problems.

In the nights Mhalsapathi and Tatya slept with Baba in the mosque. They slept in such a way that all their heads were in the centre and their legs stretched in different directions. They discussed several matters. Mostly Baba answered their questions. Sometimes Baba used to teach them about matters connected with *Atma.* Now and then Shama also joined them. Sometimes Baba used to keep Mhalsapathi's hand on his chest and ask him to put his ear close to the hand and hear the sounds that came from Baba's heart. Mhalsapathi used to hear God's "Nama japa" from Baba's heart. When he slept keeping his hand on Baba's chest, he woke him up by calling him "Arre Bhagath" and asked him to sleep properly. At any time of the night, if anyone woke up, Baba used to call him by his name. From this it is clear that Baba never slept. Though his eyes were found closed he was having only 'Yoga Sleep' as told by Mhalsapathi.

That was in the year 1886 (full-moon night) in the month of *Margashira.* At about ten in the night Baba and Mhalsapathi were discussing something. Baba was suffering from asthma and he told Mhalsapathi: "Now I will be leaving my physical body and going up. After three days I will re-enter this body. You should take good care of my body for these three days. In case I do not come back after three days, bury my body opposite to the mosque and put two flags on top." So saying Baba put his head on the thigh of Mhalsapathi and left his physical body. Tatya who came just then saw the happening and was surprised. News spread through Shirdi village that Baba died. Many gathered near the mosque. Only Tatya and Shama believed the words of Mhalsapathi who narrated what Baba had told him. Others disbelieved and thought that Baba had really died. Taking this as a good opportunity, the village *munsif* Bhate began criticising that for a person with so many divine powers, where was the need to die?

By daybreak all the villagers of Shirdi gathered before the mosque. Bhate with his followers tried to move the physical body of Baba from its place. Mhalsapathi opposed the move. Since Baba had promised to come back to his body after three days, the body should not be moved till then. Some villagers agreed with Mhalsapathi and therefore Bhate could not do anything. But he still insisted that a dead person can never come back alive, and that Mhalsapathi, out of his blind faith in Baba, was believing this and it was better to get a doctor and get the body examined. He sent for a doctor from Ahmednagar. The doctor came to Shirdi on the morning of the third day. He examined the body carefully and declared that the dead body was three days old. But there were no such symptoms of a dead body. He cautioned that as there was plague prevalent in nearby places, it was not advisable to keep the dead body thus. The villagers come to a decision that if life did not return to the body after completion of three days, then the last rites would be performed. But in the early hours of the fourth day, the body started breathing. There was movement of the limbs. In a few minutes Baba sat up. Mhalsapathi, overjoyed, said loudly, "Sri Sainath Maharaj Ki Jai"! Tatya and Shama also repeated this. Hearing all this, the villagers came to Dwarakamai and prostrated before Sai Baba.

Seeing Baba moving about, Bhate, who thought Baba to be dead, duly certified by the doctor, was so wonderstruck that he now started fully believing in Baba as the incarnation of God. From that day he became the greatest devotee of Baba and brought several people to Baba with a request to get salvation.

After this incident in 1886, Baba showed several miracles and drew several persons from far and near to Shirdi. He brought about several changes in his devotees. We shall know more about such *leelas* as we proceed further.

In fact, the miracles and *leelas* shown by Sai Baba were more from this time onwards. The life history of Sai Baba from the year 1890 to 1918, for a period of 28 years, is very important for us. All of Baba's teachings, miracles and *leelas* occurred only during this period. We pray to Sai to make us continue the *Parayana* of the remaining life history with great devotion and understanding, in correct perspective.

Om Shanti ! Shanti ! Shantihi !

CHAPTER 8

Apart from the villagers of Shirdi, people residing in distant places also began to consider Baba as God-Incarnation. After seeing Baba in the state of *Samadhi* for three days, those who used to criticise him became great devotees and those who saw him as a mad *fakir* and threw stones at him in the beginning, started coming with garlands in their hands to worship him. They chanted emotionally "Sri Satchidananda Sainath Maharaj Ki Jai!" Mhalsapathi acted as the main *pujari* for Baba. Shama also did different kinds of service to him. Bhagoji Shinde who was cured of leprosy by him, served all through Baba's life, and he was the only person who was with him at all times. He did not get into family bonds and dedicated himself to Baba's service.

Practice of 'Yogas' by Baba

There was big banyan tree, far from the mosque, towards the north. There was a well near the tree. Once in two or three days Baba went there to take his bath. One day Baba brought out his lungs from his inside by vomiting, cleaned them with water and dried them in sunlight; this was actually seen by some villagers of Shirdi. He also used to practise *dhouti,* which means cleansing the intestines. He used to swallow a piece of cloth measuring 3 inches in width and 22-1/2 inches in length, keeping it inside the stomach for half an hour. Then the cloth would stretch fully into the intestines. Afterwards he would slowly pull out the cloth, thus cleaning the inside of the intestines.

Similarly, Sai Baba used to separate all the limbs from his body and put them in different places in the mosque. One night, a devotee saw this and feared that someone might have killed Baba. He wanted to report this matter to the village *munsif,* but later he kept quiet fearing that as he would be the first to complain, the authorities would think that he had something to do with it. Unable to suppress his curiosity, he went to the mosque early in the morning and to his astonishment found Baba sitting as usual there. Then he prostrated before him. The act of separation of all the limbs of the body is called "Kanda Yoga". Similarly, he once treated some nervous ailment in the right leg, by removing the flesh over that part, rectified the affected nerves and again put back the flesh which he had cut. Perhaps, Sai Baba used to wear the long shirt covering his entire body, with a view not to exhibit such things on his body.

He used to practise all kinds of 'Yogas' from his younger days. But he had never exhibited them before anyone publicly. Now and then piercing light rays used to emanate from his eyes and hand *(Abhaya Hastha).* These light rays were very powerful and capable of curing all ailments.

In the 14 years between 1886 and 1900, Baba dragged several persons to Shirdi just like tying a thread to a sparrow and dragging it. He taught them *Bhakti, Jnana,* and *Vairagya.* The *tahsildar* of Kopargoan named Bharva, used to visit Baba frequently and got relief for several of his ailments. In this way several persons, from high officials to ordinary people from all religions and nationalities used to come to Baba, and Shirdi became a holy place of pilgrimage. For some devotees, the moment they thought of visiting Shirdi, their problems got solved. In those days there were no proper facilities for the devotees at Shirdi. For those who wanted to stay for a couple of days at threre, the only place for their stay was the open place in front of Dwarakamai and under the neem tree in Gurusthan.

Construction of Sathe Wada

It was the year 1904. Hari Vinayak Sathe was the Deputy Collector of Ahmednagar. Once he came on an official work to Kopargaon. He had heard about Sai Baba's greatness and so he went to Shirdi as he was attracted to Baba. He purchased a piece of land near Gurusthan in the year 1906 and constructed a *wada* (resting place) for the devotees, naming it Sathe Wada, which still remains with some changes.

From the year 1904, devotees had started giving *arathis* three times a day in Dwarakamai. Nana Chandorkar, a great devotee of Baba, had finalised the procedure and the songs to be sung during the *arathis*. For the afternoon *arathi* all the villagers assembled near the mosque and sometimes the mosque overflowed with the devotees. Even though thousands flocked there, Baba blessed them. No true devotee ever left Shirdi empty-handed. Some devotees thought that since Baba had not seen them nor heard their problems, how could they get relief? Baba knew their doubts and announced publicly, "Oh my devotees! You will get rewarded for the devotion and confidence you repose in me. The moment you enter Shirdi village all your worries and difficulties will be over. Those who step into Dwarakamai, irrespective of their status, will get happiness. This 'mother' is very benovolent."

Rescue of Shama from Snakebite

Once when Shama was walking on the outskirts of Shirdi village, a poisonous snake bit his little toe. Poison started to spread in his body. He was very much afraid. His friend Bala Saheb and others wanted to take him to the temple of Vittoba, where snakebites got cured. But Shama, for whom Baba was everything, wanted them to take him to Baba. On seeing Shama Baba became furious and uttered, "Do not go up. If you do so, see what I will do!" and again said, "Get out, climb down and get out!" Shama, hearing these words, thought that Baba asked him not to go up the stairs of

Dwarakamai but to get out. He was disappointed very much, since Baba who was everything to him had uttered these words. But the truth was that these words of Baba were meant for the poison inside Shama's body and not to Shama. Even before Shama was taken inside the mosque, and Baba told about the snakebite, Baba knew everything and ordered the poison to get out of Shama's body. Afterwards he went and sat near Shama and told him, "Do not fear. This *fakir* will definitely save you. Do not go here and there but go home and take rest. But do not sleep." Within a few minutes Shama got cured. The important thing we have to learn from the above incident is that Baba's words are more powerful than *mantras.* His word itself is a *Mahamantra.* So, Sai devotees who prefer to cure by *mantras* need not run after any astrologers. The astrologers can only indicate the coming difficulties, but Sai Baba, through his blessings, can get rid of those difficulties and bring happiness.

Cholera in Shirdi

In the year 1905 cholera spread to Shirdi village. Visits to and from other villages had defindled. To eradicate cholera, the village elders had put two stipulations: (1) Carts carrying firewood should not enter the village, and (2) No one should kill a goat in the village. Baba knew that these two were useless stipulations. Because of the first stipulation, there was shortage of firewood in the village. Baba ignored these stipulations. One day, a cart carrying firewood was entering the village. The villagers tried to stop it. Knowing this, Baba came to the place, and instructed the cartman to take the cart to the mosque. No one had the courage to go against Baba's instructions.

Testing the Devotion towards Guru

Baba broke the second stipulation of the village elders—that no one shall kill a goat in the village. Someone brought an aged goat to the mosque. Bade Baba was at that time present there. Sai Baba who had special regard for Bade

Baba ordered him to kill the goat with one stroke of the knife. Baba gave him daily a portion of the amount he received by way of *dakshina* from his devotees. He used to make him sit by his side at the time of smoking the pipe or taking food. Whenever Bade Baba went to other places, Baba used to accompany him up to 100 footsteps and then return to the mosque. The real name of Bade Baba was Mohammed. Such a close associate of Baba declined to kill the goat when asked by Baba. Then Baba called Shama and told him to kill the goat. Shama went to the *wada* to bring a knife, but delayed much in coming back. Thereupon, Baba ordered Kaka Saheb Dixit to kill the goat. Dixit was an orthodox Brahmin. In spite of this he took a knife, lifted and got ready to kill the goat. Immediately Baba asked him to stop and told him, "What a merciless Brahmin you are ! You are getting ready to kill the goat!" Hearing this Dixit kept aside the knife and told Baba, "Your nectar-like words are like law to us. Those words are treated as the orders of God. We always remember you. We always pray to your form. Day and night we obey your orders. We do not go into its merits when once you give an order. It is our duty to follow your orders to the last word. This is our *Dharma.* For your sake we are prepared to sacrifice everything, including this body and wealth."

Baba had done all this just to test the devotion of his pupil's towards their Guru. He also showed how many kinds of pupil were there.

There are three kinds of *shishyas* or disciples. The best kind of disciples are those who guess what their Guru wants and immediately carry it out and serve, without waiting for an order from him. The average disciples are those who carry out the orders of the Guru to the letter. The third kind of disciples are those who go on postponing carrying out the orders of their Guru and make mistakes at every step. The first two categories of disciples only can get benefits from their Guru. Nowadays there are a number of persons who feel that they are the disciples of so and so

Guru. But they belong to the last category. Once we go to Baba, we must surrender ourselves completely and offer everything we have. Then only will we come to know the real powers of Sai Baba who has come down from Kailash. Sometimes, the firm confidence we have in Baba may become shaky. That is why we should also exercise *Saburi* (waiting with utmost patience). This is also necessary for the devotee. Prayer without faith and devotion without patience are not at all useful and nobody can benefit by such type of devotion.

May Sai Baba remain in the hearts of our readers permanently! Let Sai Baba be one of their family members. Let the Sai Devotees have *shradda* (respect) and *saburi* (patience). Let Sai's protection be for the entire world. In those who read this chapter with devotion, let the tree called *Sai Bhakti* grow in their hearts into a big banyan tree which gives shade to all who come to it, without differentiation between caste and creed, rich and poor.

Om Shanti ! Shanti ! Shantihi !

CHAPTER 9

It was the year 1903. A person was charged with theft of some articles, and brought to the court of the magistrate, Dhulia. The accused told the court that Sai Baba had given him those articles. Therefore, summons were issued to Sai Baba, by the magistrate, to appear in the court to give evidence. On a suggestion from Nana Chandorkar, all the devotees prepared an appeal to the magistrate, stating that Sai Baba was a great divine personality and all of them regarded him as God and it was not proper to ask such a 'Mahatma' to appear in the court. In case the court felt that the evidence of Sai Baba was very essential, then it could send a Commissioner to Shirdi to record the evidence of Sai Baba. The court accepted the plea of the devotees and sent Nana Joshi, who was the Assistant Collector and First Class Magistrate to Shirdi to record the evidence of Sai Baba. In Shirdi no one knew that Nana Joshi was coming.

But Baba knew about this and made arrangements before Dwarakamai, by arranging tables and chairs, making it appear like a courtroom. From the questions put by the Court Commissioner and the answers given by Baba, we glean some facts about Baba. The questions and answers were as follows:

Commissioner	:	Your name?
Sai Baba	:	All call me by the name of Sai Baba.
Commissioner	:	Your father's name?
Sai Baba	:	His name was also Sai Baba.
Commissioner	:	Your Guru's name?
Sai Baba	:	Venkusa.

Commissioner	:	Your religion?
Sai Baba	:	The religion of Kabir.
Commissioner	:	Your age?
Sai Baba	:	Millions of years.
Commissioner	:	You take oath that you will tell the truth only.
Sai Baba	:	I never told any lies before and I shall never tell lies in future also.
Commissioner	:	Do you know the accused?
Sai Baba	:	There are none whom I do not know.
Commissioner	:	The accused says that he is your devotee and he knows you.
Sai Baba	:	I am with all and all are mine.
Commissioner	:	Did you give those articles to the accused?
Sai Baba	:	In this world, whoever wants anything, I give them.
Commissioner	:	What kind of right do you have over the articles given to him ?
Sai Baba	:	Everything in this world is mine. There is nothing which does not belong to me.
Commissioner	:	This is a matter of serious nature involving theft. The accused says that you have given him these articles.
Sai Baba	:	What is all this fuss? I have no connection with this affair.

The Commissioner was surprised at the answers given by Baba to all the earlier questions. But he was confused at the answer given to the last question and did not know how to decide the case. But after thinking over it for sometime he sent for the village diary and found that the accused had never visited the village and also that Sai Baba had not gone out of the village. Therefore, the statement of the accused that Baba gave him the articles was false. The accused was punished.

From the answers given by Baba to the questions of the Commissioner it was evident that there was no living being or articles unknown to Baba in this world and he had control over everything. We also learn that he never told lies under any circumstances. This is an important aspect we have to learn from him. Truth is God. In *Ramayana,* Rama was looked upon as God only because of this quality. This is how the divine words, "Satyam Vadha — Dharmam Chara" originated.

Nanda Deep

Towards the north-east of Lendi Bagh, Baba used to keep a lighted lamp. This was started by him in the year 1890. He dug a small pit in the ground and kept the lamp inside and covered the pit with a basket. As time passed by, the lamp continued to burn and two trees, one neem and another banyan, were planted on each side. Even now devotees go round the trees and the lighted lamp (Nanda Deep). Most of the devotees believe that by going round the Nanda Deep, there will not be any quarrels among wife and husband and they would lead a happy life with the blessings of Sai Baba.

Nana Chandorkar's Arrival in Shirdi

It was the year 1892. Before leaving the village, the devotees would come to Baba, touch his feet and take his permission to leave the village. One day, the village *munsif* Appa went to Baba and sought his permission to go to Kopargaon to meet the Deputy Collector who was camping there. Baba told Appa to inform the Deputy Collector, Nana Chandorkar, that Baba wanted him to come to Shirdi. Appa was surprised at this because Baba was a *fakir* in a small village, asking the Deputy Collector to come to him.

With great hesitation Appa informed Nana Chandorkar about Baba's message. But Nana Chandorkar ignored this twice or thrice. But after some days, he came to Shirdi. At the very first meeting with Baba, he felt that both of them knew each other from several births and felt very happy.

The acquaintance with Baba slowly grew and Nana Chandorkar became a staunch devotee of Baba. After personally experiencing several *leelas* of Sai Baba, Nana Chandorkar concluded that Baba was the incarnation of God.

Nana Chandorkar had one sentry named Ganapathi Rao Sahasra Bude. Against his wish, he was brought to Shirdi in the year 1893 by Nana Chandorkar and made to visit Baba. In this way Ganapathi Rao visited Baba several times and understood Baba's supernatural powers and saw his miracles. He later became famous as Das Ganu.

There is no written record of Baba's *leelas* prior to the visit of Nana Chandorkar. Having noticed this, Nana Chandorkar gave diaries to all the close devotees of Baba with a request to record whenever and whatever they noticed about his greatness, his *leelas* and miracles. The life history of Baba became possible to compile only because of the foresight of Nana Chandorkar. The various procedures for conducting *pujas,* giving *arathis,* etc., were also regulated by Nana Chandorkar. He gave lectures about Baba and made known Baba's *leelas* to the people.

Ganapathi Rao Sahasra Bude alias Das Ganu was a talented singer and actor. Throughout Maharashtra he spread Baba's stories through *Hari Kathas.* The changes brought in the life of Das Ganu by Sai Baba will be narrated in the coming chapters.

Let us pray to Sai Baba to remove our difficulties and delusions, so that we will dedicate our life towards the spreading of Sai's message (Sai Tatva), as was done by Das Ganu.

Om Shanti ! Shanti ! Shantihi !

CHAPTER 10

In the year 1898, Das Ganu (Ganapathi Rao), who was a police constable, was entrusted by the Government to catch the notorious dacoit Khana Bhill. Once or twice Khana Bhill's associates caught hold of Das Ganu but left him with pity. Das Ganu was contemplating to leave his police job and dedicate himself in the service of Sai Baba as willed by Baba. But Das Ganu thought that if he could catch the notorious dacoit, the Government would be pleased and give him promotion, which after enjoying for some time, he would leave the job and serve Baba. Khana Bhill's associates got hold of Das Ganu for the third time and they wanted to kill him. Das Ganu prayed to Baba. He took a vow that if he was saved by Baba this time, he would leave his job and dedicate himself to Baba. In an unexpected way, Khana Bhill let go Das Ganu. Afterwards Das Ganu continued in the service for some time and finally left his job in the year 1903.

The devotion to Baba started in Das Ganu in the year 1893, slowly fortified in the year 1903 when he left his job. These 10 years he used to visit Baba now and then. Baba brought about several changes in Das Ganu. He used to declare that even if his devotee was beyond the seven seas he would drag him to Shirdi in the same manner as tying a thread to the leg of sparrow and dragging it. This had come true in the case of Das Ganu. After 1903, Das Ganu spread the message of Baba throughout Maharashtra by means of *Hari Kathas*. He used to keep a big photo of Baba on the stage whenever he gave programmes. This *Hari Katha* programme used to last for four or five hours and thousands of people would attend. Similarly, Nana Chandorkar spread Baba's message through his lectures.

The Story of Maina Thai

In 1904, Nana Chandorkar was working at a place called Jamner which was about 100 miles from Shirdi. His daughter Maina Thai was in labour pains since two days and was suffering a lot. Eminent doctors came to his house and gave medical aid, but delivery did not take place and she continued to suffer unbearable pains. Then Nana Chandorkar prayed to Baba and sought his help. At the same time in Shirdi, a *sanyasi* named Ramgiri Buva sought permission of Baba to go home. Baba gave him permission and his blessings and asked him to visit Jamner on the way and hand over the *udi* and *arathi* hymn to Nana Chandorkar. But Ramgiri Buva hesitated because he had no money to go to Jamner. Baba told him not to worry and that all arrangements for his journey to Jamner would be made and asked him to proceed immediately. He used to call him Bapugiri Buva.

Having complete faith in Baba, he started for Jamner. He alighted at Jalgaon station at night at about one o'clock. The money he had with him was sufficient for the journey up to Jalgaon only. To go to Jamner he had to go by a tonga (horse-drawn carriage) for 30 miles. Not knowing what to do he sat down and prayed to Baba. At the same time a well built person was calling out "Who is Bapugiri Buva? who has come from Shirdi?" On hearing this Bapugiri Buva met him and the person informed him that Nana Chandorkar had sent the tonga. Thereupon, they proceeded in the tonga which travelled very fast. The tonga driver stopped near a rivulet and offered some eatables saying that they were sent by Nana Chandorkar. After eating them and drinking fresh water from the rivulet, they proceeded again. In the early hours before daybreak, the tonga reached the outskirts of Jamner. Babugiri Buva got out of the tonga and went to answer nature's call. When he returned he did not find the tonga or the driver. He wondered what had happened to them. He went into the village and after making enquiries reached Nana Chandorkar's house. He handed over the *udi* and the *arathi* hymn. Everybody was happy to receive the *udi* sent by Baba. Immediately they mixed it with water and made Maina Thai drink it. While they began singing the *arathi* song, Maina Thai delivered a male child.

All those present there who saw this miracle praised Baba by saying aloud "Bhagwan Sree Sainath Ki Jai!" When Bapugiri Buva thanked Nana Chandorkar for sending the tonga, Nana Chandorkar was wonderstruck and told Bapugiri Buva that he had no tonga and he had not sent anyone to the station. Bapugiri Buva concluded that it has all Baba's *leela;* it was Baba who called him by name at the Jalgaon station. Baba in the forms of horse, tonga and tonga driver simultaneously had driven him to Jamner. He experienced supreme bliss at Baba's love. So did Nana Chandorkar knowing how Baba saved his daughter. On seeing this miracle, the members of Nana Chandorkar's family and people from nearby became great devotees of Baba.

"I am spread all over this world. I do not require a tonga or cart or any other mode of travel, to come to you. If my devotee prays to me, then I shall be by his side." This charter of Baba came true in the case of Nana Chandorkar.

Baba was Akalkot Maharaj

In the year 1876 Samardha Akalkot Maharaj attained *Samadhi* in the village of Akalkot. A devotee of his was preparing to go to Akalkot in 1904. But Akalkot Maharaj appeared in his dream and told him that there was no need to come to Akalkot as he was at Shiridi in the Avatar of Sai Baba. When the devotee visited Baba, the latter blessed him and told him that Akalkot Maharaj and he are the same.

Sai Baba is not merely Akalkot Maharaj, he is also the incarnation of all gods. He appeared as Rama, Krishna, Maruti, Datta and also as Ganesh to several devotees.

Before closing this chapter, let us pray at the feet of Sai Baba who is the incarnation of all gods and protector of all, to show mercy on us, and increase our devotion towards him.

Om Shanti ! Shanti ! Shantihi !

CHAPTER 11

In the year 1896, Gopal Rao Gundu was the Revenue Inspector of Kopargaon circle. In spite of having three wives, he had no children. With the blessings of Sai Baba children were born to him. Out of gratitude to him he thought of celebrating Urs festival every year. Baba agreed to this. It was decided to celebrate the festival on Shree Ramanavami day.

Urs-Shree Ramanavami Festivals

In the year 1897 the Urs celebration was started in Shirdi for the first time on Ramanavami Day. Simultaneously the Muslim devotees started the Sandal Utsav. A devotee, Amir Shakkar, belonging to the village Korah, got the Sandal Utsav performed at Shirdi. They put sandalpaste in a big plate and took it in a procession with drums and cymbals to Dwarakamai. They smeared the walls of Dwarakamai with sandalpaste.

During the Sandal Utsav and Ramanavami Utsav, they got two flags prepared with silk cloth and zari borders; they brought them in a procession and planted them on either side of the mosque. The festival, thus started, had become a full-fledged Ramanavami festival from the year 1912 at the instance of Sree Krishna Rao Jogeshwar Bhishma. The celebrations included *Hari Kathas,* cradle function and spraying coloured powder called *gulal* on one another. Next day, they hung a pot from a considerable height. This pot contained curds, riceflakes, etc. Whoever tried to catch it was sprayed with water jets. Baba moved among all the devotees, blessing them. People thought that Lord Ram a had come in the form of Sai Baba. Baba used to cry aloud with anger whenever the *gulal* powder fell in his eyes. Actually those cries were directed against the evil spirits moving around there.

After the festivities were over, Gopal Rao Gundu wanted to get the mosque repaired and put stone slabs for the flooring of Dwarakamai. But Baba gave away the stone slabs to the temples in the village for undertaking repairs.

Vasu Devananda Saraswathi

In a 'Tapovan' near Rajahmundry in Andhra Pradesh, there was a great saint with divine and supernatural powers. He was Vasu Devananda Saraswathi. Thousands of devotees visited him. Das Ganu, a native of Nanded, along with four others went to visit this *Yogi.* After hearing about Shirdi and the name of Sai Baba from Das Ganu, Vasu Devananda was overwhelmed with joy and told them, "Children! My elder brother is there in Shirdi. Why did you come here instead of visiting him? People are under the impression that Sai Baba is a Muslim *fakir*. But he is my elder brother. Please give this coconut to him with my salutations." So saying he gave a coconut to Das Ganu. They returned with Das Ganu to Nanded and after fifteen days started for Shirdi via Manmad and Kopargaon. After reaching Manmad they learnt that the train to Kopargaon was running late. So they sat near the rivulet nearby, to eat the fried riceflakes brought by them. As they found the riceflakes too pungent, they broke the coconut given to them by Vasu Devananda Saraswathi and after Crating it, mixed it with the riceflakes and ate it. While eating they suddenly remembered that this coconut was intended for Sai Baba and feared the consequences.

When they reached Shirdi, Sai Baba called Das Ganu and asked him about the coconut given by Vasu Devananda. Surprised as to how Baba knew about it, Das Ganu narrated everything and sought the pardon of Baba.

He rose to go to the shop to get another coconut. But Baba prevented him and told him, "Child, do not go. Can the coconut which you intend to bring now be equal to the one sent by my brother? Do not worry. You are also my children. All my possessions are yours. I do not have anything against you". So saying, he blessed them.

Dixit Wada

Kaka Saheb Dixit heard about the miracles and *leelas* of Sai Baba and came to Shirdi for the first time in the year 1909. While in England, his leg was injured in a train mishap and so he came to Shirdi with the hope that Baba would cure him. But after visiting Baba he prayed to Baba to make him emotionally stable rather than physically.

He saw the miracles and *leelas* of Sai Baba and decided to permanently settle down at Shirdi. He purchased a piece of land to the north of Gurusthan and constructed a rest house. He kept the first floor for himself while the ground floor was for the visiting devotees. This building was called Dixit Wada.

Bala Saheb Mireekar

Bala Saheb Mireekar was the *tahsildar* of Kopargaon. On his way to the village Chitili, he came to Shirdi to visit Sai Baba. He went inside the mosque and after salutation to Baba, sat by his side. Baba told him, "The place where you are sitting now is Dwarakamai. The mother is very kind-hearted. She is more than a mother to sincere devotees. Those real devotees who sit in her lap are relieved of their difficulties and anxieties." So saying he put his hand in the shape of a snake's hood, warning him that the snake was very dangerous. But as long as Dwarakamai protected her children, the snake could do no harm to you.

After sometime, when Bala Saheb got up to leave the mosque, Baba called Shama and ordered him to accompany Bala Saheb to Chitili. Though Bala Saheb did not agree to this, yet Baba told him, "We wish for your good. But who can change one's fate?" Reluctantly Bala Saheb agreed to Shama coming with him.

They took rest in the Hanuman temple near Chitili at about 9 o'clock in the night. Bala Saheb read the newspaper. Shama noticed a snake on the upper cloth of Bala Saheb. Bala Saheb was very frightened. The snake slid down and slithered away. The nearby people gathered there and killed the snake. Baba had foreseen this and cautioned Mireekar, also assuring him that nothing would happen. Furthermore, he had sent Shama with him for his protection.

When we pray to Baba and seek his protection, he foresees our coming difficulties and gives us the required protection, and with his blessings reduces the intensity of our difficulties. According to the theory of Karma if one had to undergo the difficulties, Baba would lessen the difficulties and alleviate our suffering. In the above story, there must have been danger from snakebite for Bala Saheb as per the Theory of Fate. But Baba's assurance to Bala Saheb was more powerful, and though the snake went up the upper cloth of Bala Saheb it could not do anything. Some devotees fully believed in Sai Baba, but no miracles or *leelas* happened to them and Sai Baba did not do anything for them. But Sai Baba foresaw their difficulties and tried to prevent them. In the eighth chapter we had seen how Baba had saved Shama from snakebite, by ordering the poison to come down. From these stories, the readers can imagine how Baba protects his devotees with his motherly love.

The Need for a Guru

In any *Yuga,* the need for a Guru was there for spiritual advancement. Lord Rama and Lord Krishna, regarded as incarnations of God, also had Gurus. Any high caste person or wealthy or strong person or a person with knowledge of the *Vedas,* etc., cannot have spiritual advancement unless he has a Guru. Mere book knowledge is not sufficient to know the path of God-realisation. A Sadguru will be useful for us like a guide in a forest. We shall now learn about this in Baba's words.

One day Dixit came to Baba and sought permission to leave Shirdi. Baba gave him his permission. Someone there asked, "Where to?" and Baba said, "To a place very far up. There are several ways to reach that place. From Shirdi also there is a way. This is a very difficult one. There are tigers, wolves, etc., in the forest. If you take a guide along with you, he will safely take you to your destination, making you escape from the wild animals. If there is no guide accompanying you, you can get killed by the wild animals, or you may fall in some pit. You can get salvation only by the Guru's teachings."

The gist of Baba's teaching is that life's journey is like travelling through a thick forest. Jealousy, selfishness and hatred will infest this jungle like wild animals. We do not know which moment we may fall prey to them. To move forward avoiding these pitfalls, the help of a Sadguru is very essential.

Shirdi Sai Baba is the incarnation of Lord Shiva, come down to this world from Kailash to show the materialistic people the *Jnana Marga* and the way to salvation. It is not at all difficult to have the blessings of the Sadguru. Baba said, "If you look to me, I look to you.... If you come one step towards me, I will come ten steps towards you.... I shall give you help or advise, the moment you ask for it." Even after leaving the physical body, Sai Baba remained in this world in the form of Guru.

All Sai devotees should consider him as their Sadguru. He is the form of all gods in one. He is the creator and preserver of this world. Let us put everything at his feet and benefit from this human birth.

Das Ganu's Holy Bath

On Shivarathri day in the year 1905 Das Ganu wanted to bathe in the nearby Godavari river, and sought the permission of Baba. Baba told him, "Why should you go to such a distant place? Godavari water is at my feet." Das Ganu knew that Baba was the incarnation of Lord Shiva and Ganga Devi would be always with him. But he thought that the satisfaction of bathing in a river would not be there. Knowing the thoughts inside Das Ganu, Baba asked him to hold both the palms of his hands together and put them near his feet. When Das Ganu did this, holy water flowed from the toes of Baba's feet. Wonderstruck at this, Das Ganu sprinkled the water on his head with joy and got the satisfaction of having bathed in River Ganga.

Isha Upanishad

Das Ganu was not able to understand the gist of *Isha Upanishad* and therefore approached many persons who too could not explain it to him properly. Thereupon he decided to go to Shirdi and take the help of Sai Baba in understanding the *Upanishad* properly. Baba blessed him and told him not to be in a hurry to know the gist, saying, "In your return journey, if you go to the house of Kaka Saheb Dixit at Ville Parle, his servant girl will clear your doubts." The other devotees there wondered how an illiterate servant girl could clear his doubts when so many learned people could not do this. But Das Ganu took Baba's words as divine truth.

On his return journey he stayed in the house of Dixit. He found the servant girl wearing a torn dress and singing happily and attending to the household work. He wondered at the poor servant girl in such a happy mood. He presented a saree to her through his friend Pradhan. The servant girl wore the new saree and sang and danced with joy with other girls. Next day she put her new saree in her box and came to work with the torn dress that she had earlier worn. But there was no change in her behaviour. She was as happy as she was when wearing the new saree. After observing this, Das Ganu realised that sorrows and happiness depend on one's own moods and thinking and this was the central idea of *Isha Upanishad.* In this world everything is the creation of Ishwar. But according to one's mind and thought, one is happy when one has what one wants and unhappy when it is not with one. The cause of sorrow and happiness is one's mind and thinking and not the creator Ishwar.

What Gautama Buddha realised, sitting under the Bodhi Tree was only the above truth. For those who have conquered their minds there will not be sorrow but only happiness. He would always be a contented and happy person. This is the state called Brahmananda.

Today Sai Baba is not with us in flesh and blood. Then how will he teach us *Jnana.* This question may be in your mind. The way how he taught Das Ganu through a servant girl, in the same manner Baba would also teach us *Jnana* through our own actions and through the actions of the people around us. But we should have the true desire and understanding capacity. Sai Baba will give us these qualities only if we surrender ourselves completely to him.

Sai Baba will be observing how far you are able to assimilate anything while doing *Parayana* of his life history. When you have devotion to Baba and are sincere in the *Parayana,* everything will automatically be grasped by our minds. Then Baba will show his *leelas.* So, if you want to experience the love of Baba towards you, you should do *Parayana* in the above mentioned manner. This is something you yourself have to practise where others cannot help.

Let us end this chapter with a prayer to Sai Baba to impart *Jnana* to those who read his life history with devotion and also to stay in their hearts permanently and make their houses a Sai Nilayam.

Om Shanti ! Shanti ! Shantihi !

CHAPTER 12

The actions of Baba seems impossible to believe sometimes and at times strange. No one understands why Baba did thus.

Baba's Strange Actions

In the early days when the holy fire (Dhuni) was started in Dwarakamai, Baba collected used matchsticks and stored them carefully. He took *dakshina* half-anna (equivalent to three paise) from the devotees who visited him. He smoked from a mudpipe called *chillum.*

With thin and weak cloth pieces measuring five feet in length and one and half feet in width, Baba used to hang a wooden board four inches thick, to the rafters of Dwarakamai. He put four lamps at the four corners of the wooden board, and slept on the board. While it was surprising as to how the cloth pieces withstood the weight of the wooden board, it was more surprising as to how they withstood the weight of Baba also.

In the afternoons, between 1 and 2 p.m. devotees were not allowed inside the mosque. During this period Baba would take out 15 to 20 old coins from his bag and rub them with his fingers, saying aloud, "This coin is Nana's, this coin is Kaka's." Perhaps by doing like this Baba was removing their desires.

Everyday, after watering the plants in Lendi Bagh, Baba would put the earthen pots with their mouths down. Once a person named Kolambi, observing this crazy action of Baba, asked him why he was doing like that. To this Baba replied that people who were coming to him were like the earthen pots with their mouths down, meaning they were not able to receive carefully what Baba wanted to give them.

Baba's Knowledge of Past, Present and Future (Ruthambara Prajna)

Baba used to tell his devotees frequently:

"Whether you are before me or at far off place, whatever you do and think will be known to me." He used to tell the devotees who visited him, their past, present and future. This is called Ruthambara Prajna in *Yoga Shastra.* This is found in saints in a limited capacity. But Baba's power was limitless, covering the entire world and beyond imagination.

Baba sometimes brought to life some persons who were dead. But he did not revive some persons. One day a woman, whose child died, came to Baba and asked for *udi.* In spite of her repeated pleas, he declined to give it. When Kaka Saheb Dixit intervened in the matter Baba told him "Baav! Do not interfere in this matter. Whatever happened has happened for the good. The dead boy has already taken birth in another body in which he will do many good things. If I bring the boy here now, the new body will perish and this body will live. If I do this for your sake, will you accept the consequential responsibility ?"

Baba would immediately answer any question that was put to him. Though the answer appeared to be coincidental, his word turned into absolute truth. Though he would appear to be seeing and talking like us, he would always be in a state of *Samadhi.* He was a confirmed bachelor like Hanuman. Lust feared to approach him. His eyes were like burning lamps and penetrated like searchlights the hearts of many.

How Baba saved Nana Chandorkar

Baba always looked after those who believed in him. One day, Chandorkar and his friend Shastri were travelling in a *tonga* from Poona. Suddenly the horse pushed back the *tonga* with the result that the *tonga* fell upside down. Both men fell down. This was a serious accident. In the ordinary course there was danger to the life of the passengers. At the same hour at Shirdi, putting his hands together like a conch Baba made sounds like that emanating from a conch. It was an indication of imminent danger. Baba cried aloud, "Nana is falling down! But I will not let it happen." Because of this *leela* Nana and his friend escaped unhurt and completed their journey safely.

One day, Nana Chandorkar was climbing the Harischandra hill to see a temple there. Another friend and two servants accompanied him. After climbing for sometime, he felt very thirsty due to severe heat from the sun. Becoming tired he rested. There was no water nearby. To get water, either one had to go down or else go up the hill. He remembered Baba. He thought that if Baba were to be here, he would have somehow provided him water. But he was 80 miles away at Shirdi. At the same hour, Baba, sitting in Dwarakamai told Shama and others, "Nana is very thirsty. The climate is very hot. He was also tired. I should give him some water." Shama and others could not understand what Baba said.

On the hill, Nana sat silently for sometime. A Bhil (of the forest-dwelling tribe) happened to come there. Coming near Nana he told him that if he was thirsty, water could be had from the water hole under the big stone on which he was sitting. When the stone was shifted, pure drinking water was found. Nana quenched his thirst by drinking the water. After some days when Shama told Chandorkar what Baba had said a few days back, he recollected the incident and concluded that Baba himself had come in the form of the Bhil to quench his thirst.

Baba taught Nana about Mind Control

One day, a Muslim family from Bijapur came to visit Baba. There were two ladies in their veils. They came to Baba, and removing their veils saluted him. One of the ladies was very beautiful. Nana was sitting next to Baba and at the sight of the beautiful lady, his mind went astray. He wished to see her face again. Observing this Baba hit him gently on the thigh. After the ladies left Baba asked Nana if he know why he had hit him. Nana replied that having noticed his agitated mind, Baba must have hit him. Baba said, "The lady you saw was very beautiful. God has created her so beautifully. When a person created by God is so beautiful, then how much more beautiful would be the creator? Did you ever think of this?"

We should always think of the creator of this beautiful world and not the things created. We go to a temple to worship God and not to see the sculptures. When mind merges with senses then only one gets excited. Our body is like a chariot. The mind is the driver *(sarathi)* and the senses are horses. If the charioteer holds the reins firmly, then one can safely reach one's destination. Instead, if the charioteer loses control over the horses they would run wildly and one cannot reach one's destination. Those who can control their senses with mind, alone can advance spiritually. Those who become slaves to the senses, will use their mind only to achieve their desires. If we tempt the senses with anything, they will desire to have it. Because of this nature of the senses, you desired to see that lady again and again. You can stop that desire by controlling with your mind. Then you can utilise all your leisure time for spiritual purposes. Otherwise, the entire life time will be spent on achieving our desires, and where then is the time to think of God?"

Baba's Control over all the Five Elements

The entire world is made up of five elements (i) earth (ii) water (iii) fire (iv) air, and (v) sky. This was known to Indians even before the ancient *Puranas.* According to the latest science, the entire creation is a combination of one or more of these elements. Baba had full control over these elements. There were several instances to prove this.

One day, there was a heavy downpour in Shirdi due to cyclonic conditions. The roofs of some thatched houses were about to be blown off. There was knee-deep water in the entire village. All the villagers young and old came to the mosque and pleaded with Baba to save them. The kind-hearted Baba came out of the mosque and commanded the wind and rain to reduce their intensity by saying "Stop! Slow down!" In a few minutes, the rains stopped. In the same way, Baba stopped the rain on an earlier occasion when Nana Chandorkar wanted to return home.

One day the flames in the Dhuni in the mosque, went high up all of a sudden touching the wooden rafters. Then Baba, striking the floor with his *sataka,* ordered the flames to come down. On one summer day the haystock of a farmer caught fire, and was burning, assisted by the blowing wind. There was not sufficient water in the village to put out the fire. All feared that the flames would spread to the neighbouring haystacks and to the nearby houses. Some ran to Sai Baba and begged him to save them from the calamity. Immediately, Baba went to the raging fire and with a small vessel containing water sprinkled it around the haystack and ordered the fire not to go beyond that boundary. The fire subsided after sometime without spreading.

In the first year of the celebration of Ramanavami in Shirdi, there was acute water shortage. To tide over this shortage, Baba threw flowers into the dried up village well. Immediately water oozed and filled the well. This is another instance to prove Baba's control over the elements.

Megashyam, a native of Vivergaon, was the Brahmin cook of Sathe. He was a very orthodox person. In the early days of Sathe's visit to Shirdi, Megashyam was given the work of a *pujari* and also to serve Baba. Over a period, Megashyam saw several of Baba's *leelas* and fully believed that Baba was the incarnation of Lord Shiva. He used to daily drink the water with which Baba's feet were washed.

Baba brought about a change in him and made his devotion permanent.

On one Shankranthi, Meghashyam wanted to apply sandalpaste all over Baba's body and bathe the body with Ganga water (water from nearby Godavari river). He sought permission of Baba who reluctantly gave it. He walked to and fro 18 miles and brought the water in a pot on his head. It was noon time. He made Baba sit on a low wooden stool. Baba put his head a little forward and told Megashyam that since the head was the important part of the body, it was enough if the water was put on his head only instead of on the entire body. But Megashyam crying out ecstatically "Har Ganga" emptied the water from the pot on the entire body. But to his surprise, Baba's advise, only Baba's head got wet as Baba desired.

From the above two *leelas,* it is evident that Baba had complete control over water also.

Brahma Jnana

A very rich man Gulzar was residing near Malegaon. On hearing about the powers and *leelas* of Sai Baba, he decided to go to Shirdi to get *Brahma Jnana* from Baba. He engaged a tonga for the journey. After reaching Shirdi, he approached Baba, and asked him to teach him *Brahma Jnana* without delay, as he had engaged a tonga for the journey. Baba told him, "Friend, do not get worried. I will show you Brahman just now. All my transactions are for cash only and no account. All who come to me are with selfish desires. Very few ask for *Brahma Jnana* like you." So saying, Baba diverted the topic. He called for a boy and asked him to get five rupees as loan from Nandu Marwadi. The boy returned after sometime stating that the house was locked. Baba sent him to some other house, with the same result. He sent him to two more places, but without succees. Then Baba looked at Gulzar who had come for Brahma *Jnana,* and said, "There are fifty currency notes of five rupees denomination in your pocket. Attaining *Brahma Jnana* urgently is not materialistic.

I have been sending the boy to get a loan of five rupees, with the intention that you should observe. You did not volunteer to give that five rupees to me, that too as a loan, even though you have a lot of money. Such a miser cannot understand *Brahma Jnana.* You were in a hurry because, if there was delay the *tongawala* would charge you more."

Baba then added, "Oh friend! *Brahma Jnana* means realisation of Self *(Atma).* There is no difference between *Atma* and God. If you want to realise *Atma* in your body, then you have to surrender to God the following five things: (1) five pranas (2) five senses (3) mind (4) intellect and (5) ego. All these are inside a person. It is easy to surrender the external things. But to surrender those which are inside a person is very difficult. It is like walking on the edge of a sharp knife. Those who cannot surrender even the external things are deemed to be fully under delusion. Such persons cannot understand the five inside matters.

"A person who wants Self-realisation or *Atma Jnana,* should be careful in the following matters:

"1. A strong desire should be there for *moksha* or freedom from worldly matters.

"2. One should have detachment from all things of this world and also desires about the other world *(paraloka).*

"3. All the senses of a man are accustomed to seeing external things only. One should make these senses see the self or *Atma.*

"4. When he cannot divert his mind from bad and undesirable things and not be able to control his mind, he cannot get *Atma-Sakshatkara* even if he gets *Jnana.*

"5. One should always speak the truth under all circumstances and remain a bachelor.

"6. Man should choose only that which will do him good and not that which gives him pleasure. Worldy matters give pleasure. Spiritual matters do him good.

Instead of going for temporary or momentary pleasures, one should prefer spiritual matters only, which do good to him.

"7. Man should have under control, the mind and sensory organs. If he goes in for pleasures, the senses also will keep the mind occupied with these matters and there will not be any room for spiritual matters.

"8. He must keep his mind pure. He should do his duties in a proper and satisfactory way, without expecting reward for his actions. Then the mind will be pure. Knowledge comes out from a purified mind and increases detachment, leading to self-realisation. Unless greed, delusions and desires are removed, man cannot get *Jnana.*

"9. If all the above-mentioned thing are practised rigorously he will achieve results. After this stage, the need for a 'Guru' arises. A Guru should be one who has attained *Atma-Jnana,* otherwise no useful purpose will be served.

"10. The first eight are one's own efforts. To this, if the help of a Sadguru is also there, then God's blessings will also be there. Knowledge of the *Vedas,* or riches or great intelligence will not get us *Atma-Jnana.*"

The above lengthy speech of Baba was not only directed to Gulzar but to all other Sai devotees and readers of this life history. May the readers do *parayana* of the portion of this chapter dealing with *Brahma Jnana.* Those who read this with devotion will have Sai Baba as their Sadguru permanently. Let their lives journey be towards *Atma Sakshatkara.*

What are the needs of a man? Happiness, peace, food and clothing and bodily requirements. Sai Baba has said, "In my devotees house, nothing will be wanting." So we should not waste our life for the sake of food and clothing, name and fame. Attachments to mother, father, brother, wife, husband, etc., are limited to this birth only, but the attachment to Sai will be there for several births *(janmas)* to come.

Let us wish that through the *parayana* of this sacred *Life History of Sai Baba,* Sai will be a part of our family and our lives shall be tied up with Sai Baba.

Om Shanti ! Shanti ! Shantihi !

End of Second Day's Parayan

THIRD DAY'S PARAYAN—SATURDAY

CHAPTER 13

Mhalsapathi

It was the year 1895. After experiencing Baba's supernatural powers and his love, Mhalsapathi was fully drawn to Baba and become detached from worldly attachments. One night, Khandoba appeared in his dream and asked, "If you do not do your traditional gold-smith work, cannot you get food?" To this Mhalsapati replied, "If I have your compassion then there won't be anything wanting and I will leave my work." From that day Mhalsapathi left his traditional work and became an ascetic, living only on alms.

Gradually he developed a detachment from family. He went home only for taking food. At all other times he was serving Baba. He slept in the mosque with Baba during nights. In the following year, one day Baba said, "Bhagat, hear the words of this *fakir*. You are sleeping in the nights in the mosque. Go and sleep in your house. You have three children, all daughters. A son will be born. Go and sleep in your house."

Mhalsapathi had no desire for having a son. In fact, he had no desires at all. So he did not follow Baba's orders. Baba forcibly sent him home with his friend Kasiram Shimpe on Krishna Jayanti day. On the same day the following year exactly after a year, a son was born to him. Baba's words had come true. The boy was named

Marthand. When this boy grew up to the school-going age, he refused to go to school one day. When Mhalsapathi tried to beat him, the boy ran to Dwarakamai and sat in the lap of Baba. Mhalsapathi came there and beating the boy, tried to send him to school. Then Baba told Mahalsapathi with compassion, "Mhalsa, do not worry about your son. I will take good care of him."

Marthand grew up and by the name of Marthand Maharaj used to sit by the side of Mhalsapathi *Samadhi* in Shirdi. When this author met him in 1985 he narrated the above incident and said that Sai Baba had kept his word feeding him in the form of his devotees. He also said that Baba had told Mhalsapathi about his own parents, their names and birthplace. Because of the differences between Hindus and Muslims in those days, these particulars were kept secret. He added that his father had given him the details but taken an oath from him that he would not reveal them. He expired in 1986.

Now let's see how Baba saved Mhalsapathi and his family. One night when Mhalsapathi was going home to take his meal, Baba cautioned him. "Bhagat, on your way you will encounter two tall thieves. Be careful." Mhalsapathi found two snakes, one in front and one by the side of his house. Similarly on another occasion Baba cautioned him, "Bring a lantern with you. On the way you will encounter a thief." When Mhalsapathi came with the lantern, he found a snake near the mosque and he cried out, "Snake! Snake!" On hearing his cries the villagers came running and killed the snake.

Sometime in the year 1908, all the family members of Mhalsapathi fell sick. A doctor who had come to worship Baba, gave them medicines. But Baba told him that these medicines were of no use and that he would cure them of their illness. So saying, to took his *sataka* made rounds around Dwarakamai saying at the top of his voice, "Come— I shall see how powerful you are!" Soon all the family members of Mhalsapathi recovered from their illness. Baba's action might have been against the diseases in the house of Mhalsapathi.

Once Mhalsapathi's wife went to her parents' house. There she had an attack of throat infection due to which suffered a lot. At Shirdi, Baba told Mhalsapathi, "Your wife is suffering a lot from throat infection. Except me none can save her." Then Mhalsapathi told Baba "It is true. Except you who else in this world can save us?" Mhalsapathi had complete faith in Baba, showing it in his words and actions. Because of this Baba cured the ailment of Mhalsapathi's wife.

Even now Sai Baba saves his devotees who completely believe in him and surrender to him, as Mhalsapathi did. We appeal to the readers to do the same. Sai Baba expects pure devotion and belief and not the methods or mode of worship.

Mhalsapathi used to go every year to a village called Jijuri which was 150 miles away from Shirdi, where a festival was held for Khandoba. One year there was an epidemic of plague in that village and Mhalsapathi halted halfway from the village, very much disappointed. Baba appeared before him for a moment. He fell down at Baba's feet and when he got up Baba disappeared. He went to Jijuri and returned without any difficulties. When he went to Baba on his return, Baba questioned him, "Bhagat, Why were you disappointed during your pilgrimage. I came near your cart. Did you notice me?"

On another occasion, when Mhalsapathi wanted to go to a village, Doarhali, to attend a dinner at the house of his daughter's in-laws, Baba did not give his consent. But Mhalsapathi, thinking that the relatives may misunderstand him, went to their house. But he returned without eating after being put to some indignities. On his return he went to Baba and putting his head at his feet, started weeping. On some other occasion, Mhalsapathi wanted to go to the village Ardhangonu. But Baba did not permit him to go, as there would be clashes and disputes there. But Mhalsapathi went. As Baba had predicted there were quarrels among the village children which led to the elders entering the fray and spliting the groups into two and fighting with sticks. But Mhalsapathi escaped without any injury and returned safely.

The way Baba protected Mhalsapathi at every stage shows how Sai Baba loves his devotees. In this manner, a Guru who has the capability to look after his devotees and give protection to them, can only be called Samartha Sadguru.

Chavadi

Sometimes Baba used to go to Gurusthan, and closing his eyes merge his thoughts with those of his Guru Venkusa who resided inside the underground structure in the form of a light *(jyoti).* On hearing his disciple, Venkusa would enter the head of Baba. The Guru and disciple would silently converse. In the same manner, in Dwarakamai during nights, Baba would converse with his father Gurudhan (Ganga Bhavajya). In front of the mosque there was a big hall, where sadhus (mendicants) took rest and it was called Chavadi. The *sadhus* and *sanyasis* who came to the village stayed there.

Nana Chandorkar and some others made all arrangements to tile the floor in Dwarakamai. They requested Baba to sleep in the Chavadi for a night, so that they could attend to the laying of tiles in Dwarakamai overnight. Baba agreed and went to the Chavadi. He sat alone there, as Tatya and Mhalsapathi also were busy with tile-laying work. No one else was with Baba in the Chavadi. In a meditative mood he concentrated on Dwarakamai, Gurudhan and Venkusa. The three appeared before him in the form of *jyotis.* They discussed several matters. After sometime Gurudhan and Dwarakamai went back to their places. Baba and Venkusa discussed things that would take place in Shirdi in future and also for the next 500 years. In the meantime twilight broke and Venkusa prepared to leave. But Baba pleaded with Venkusa to remain in the Chavadi and that he would come there on alternate days. Venkusa, out of love for Baba, agreed to remain on the right side portion of the Chavadi saying that women should not be allowed to enter that place. Baba agreed to this and from that day onwards till today Venkusa is there in Chavadi in an invisible form.

Baba, living in the lap of his mother (Dwarakamai) and attracting his father through whom he got this birth taught his disciples *Jnana,* he gave salvation to those who approached him, and became the God of this Kaliyuga which had set in the Sai Yuga. Sai Baba bade goodbye to orthodox ways of worship and other practices. In this connection Sai Baba said, "Those who are lucky and those whose sins have been atoned will worship me. I will help them to even cross the seven seas who always think of my name. I am not interested in their ways of worship and other practices. I will dwell in the hearts of those who have sacred devotion towards me." What he did to such devotees is recounted below now.

Greatness of Baba's Words

In the year 1909 Bhimaji Patil was suffering from tuberculosis. On the advise of Nana Saheb he came to Shirdi and fell at the feet Baba. In the beginning, though Baba declined to save him, he yielded to repeated requests from Bhimaji and taking pity on him said, "Do not fear. Your difficulties are over. Even persons with dangerous ailments will get relief once they climb up the stairs of the mosque. The *fakir* (meaning Baba) is very compassionate. He will save all with love and compassion." After Baba gave these assurances the disease of Bhimaji got cured slowly and in a few days he fully recovered and became healthy. After that Baba appeared to him in dreams twice. In the first dream it was a teacher beating him. In the second dream it was a big boulder put on his chest, and he suffered on account of this.

By beating and putting a heavy weight on the chest, Baba removed his misdeeds and restored complete health. Noticing the divine power of Sai Baba, Bhimaji Patil, after going back to his village, started performing Sai Satya Vratam on the lines of Satyanarayana Vratam for the first time.

Datta Pant was a resident of Hardha. He was suffering from severe stomach pain for the last fourteen years. He used several medicines but did not get relief. Hearing Baba's greatness, he came to Shirdi, fell at his feet and requested him to save him. Baba looked at him with compassion, blessed him and put his hand *(Abhaya Hastha)* on his head. Then he gave him *udi* as *prasad.* Datta Pant's stomach pain was cured immediately and it never recurred.

Another devotee of Baba, Kaka Mahajani, though suffering from diarrhoea, was still serving Baba. He kept water in a small vessel in the mosque, so that he could go out whenever necessary. Since Baba knew everything, Kaka believed Baba himself would cure his diarrhoea. The work of putting stones in front of the mosque had started. Suddenly, Baba opening his eyes wide yelled loudly. All those inside the mosque ran out, out of fear. Kaka Mahajani was also trying to run out. But Baba caught hold of his hand and made him sit down. He gave him some groundnuts, left by someone, and asked him to eat them. Baba also ate some. He asked Kaka to drink some water. After sometime he told him that his diarrhoea was cured and he could attend to the work of laying stones in front of the mosque. Kaka noticed that the diarrhoea had stopped. Only Baba could have cured Kaka's diarrhoea and none else.

On another occasion, Nana Saheb Chandorkar suffered from stomach pain. In spite of taking many medicines, he could not got relief. He came to Shirdi and approached Baba. With Baba's hand raised in blessing, the stomach pain subsided completely.

Another of Baba's devotees, Bala Ganapathi Shimpe, was suffering from malaria. He tried several medicines but did not get relief. So he came to Shirdi and approached Baba. Baba asked him to go to Lakshmi Mandir and offer curds and rice to the black dog in front of the temple. As per Baba's advise he took the curd and rice to Lakshmi Mandir. There he noticed a black dog wagging its tail and appeared as if waiting for him. He gave the curd-rice to the black dog, which ate it completely. The *malarial* fever subsided and he once again became healthy.

Bapu Saheb Buty once suffered from vomiting and diarrhoea. Being a wealthy person he tried several medicines which gave no relief. Having become very weak, he could not even go to see Baba. But Baba himself sent for him and asked him to sit before him. Enlarging his eyes in a serious manner, Baba looking into Buty's eyes and cautioned "You should not vomit or pass stools." Immediately Buty got relief and became healthy.

A *sanyasi* from Allandi came to see Baba. He was suffering from severe pain in the ear. Having noticed this, Shama pleaded with Baba on behalf of the sanyasi to cure his pain. Baba said, " Allaha *achcha karega,"* meaning God will do good. So saying, Baba raised his hand in blessing and shifted his looks towards the sanyasi for a moment. The *sanyasi* got immediate relief.

Only a few incidents out of thousands are given above. It can be seen that Baba's words were more powerful than the medicines. His words were the words of God. Only such a person can be called Sadguru. The other gurus show more interest in the money brought by disciples and also other material things they bring. But they can in no way useful to their disciples. Instead of going to such gurus and wasting precious time, the readers are advised to believe in Sai Baba and attain salvation.

Om Shanti ! Shanti ! Shantihi !

CHAPTER 14

It was the year 1906. The day was *Vyasa Poornima* in the month *Ashada.* It was called Vyasa Poornima in recognition of Vyasa Maharshi, who authored the eighteen Puranas. On the morning of this day, Baba called Kelkar, Sathe's father-in-law, and told him that this day was *Guru Poornima,* when the Guru was to be worshipped. He asked him to bring Shama and other devotees along with the *puja* materials. Dada Kelkar collected all the devotees and with the *puja* materials, brought them to the mosque. By then, Baba with this half-closed eyes was concentrating on something. Noticing this no one had the courage to talk to him for fear of disturbing his concentration. After a while, Baba opened his eyes, looked at the devotees for a moment and fell silent again.

Till then everyone believed that Baba was the incarnation of God, with divine and supernatural powers but no one had the thought to worship Baba as their 'Guru'. Hence, they did not know whom they should worship as Guru and how to worship, and kept quiet. Knowing their thoughts Sai Baba taught them as follows.

"You are all worshipping me as a *fakir* with divine and supernatural powers. Some of you are believing that I am the incarnation of God. Allah *Malik hai.* I am only his servant. I am like a father to you all. You should benefit from me. I have come into this world to divert your thoughts from materialism towards spiritualism, and establish truth, righteousness, peace and love in you and through you to the entire mankind, and bless them with peace and happiness. This is the goal of Sai Avatar. If you worship me keeping me in a photoframe like other gods, you will not benefit anything from me. But you should consider me as your 'Guru' and surrender completely to me and put into practice what all I teach you. Your present actions only are the foundations for your future lives and births. You should all treat today's *Vyasa Poornima* as *Guru Poornima* and worship me as your Guru and make your lives happy."

Guru Poornima

From among all the devotees who had gathered in the mosque, Dada Kelkar went to Baba, prostrated before him, washed his feet in a plate, took a little of this water *(Pada Tirtha)* inside and sprinkled it on his head, distributing it to all those present. After this he put sandalpaste on Baba's forehead, put a dot with *kumkum* and worshipped him with flowers and *akshatas* (rice). Then he broke a coconut and gave *arathi* with camphor. While the *arathi* was being given, Baba's face became very bright as if a thousand lamps were lighted with different colours. The surprised devotees wanted to touch Baba's feet and prostrate before him. Noticing the thoughts of the devotees, he slowly walked towards the big stone that he created in front of Dwarakamai, while the devotees spread flowers all the way and made him walk on the flowers. As soon as he reached the stone he sat on it putting his left hand on the toe of his right leg and putting the right hand on the thigh of his right leg. Then he looked deeply into the eyes of each devotee, by which the joy experienced by them was beyond description. When they touched his feet, they felt an unknown divine power entering their bodies and reach their hearts. These things have to be personally experienced and cannot be explained. All those who experienced this, started to celebrate *Guru Poornima* on every *Ashada Suddha Poornima* day with pomp and gaiety. Even today *Guru Poornima* is celebrated in Shirdi. This festival is very important to Sai devotees as they worship their Guru according to their might and get the blessings from him. Those who worship their Guru with devotion and sincerity on this day, will always have the Guru with them. Sai Baba had personally told them that he was Sadguru and they could not get another Guru in this world. We should completely surrender ourselves to him and seek *Jnana Marga.* For those who read this chapter with devotion, let their mind grow and get true vision.

Om Shanti ! Shanti ! Shantihi !

CHAPTER 15

In the tenth chapter we learnt how Baba saved Maina Tai from her sufferings during delivery, by sending her *udi.* In this chapter we will know some more incidents showing the greatness of *udi.* By giving it as *prasad* to the devotees, what did Baba intend to convey? "Everything in this world will end as ash. When life goes out of our bodies, they are cremated and they turn into ash. For such a short-lived body's sake, why do you indulge in greed, deceit, sins and desires?" To make the devotees realise that everything in this creation is transient including the body which is finally reduced into ash, Baba gave *udi.* Now let us see how this *udi* worked.

Greatness of Udi

One Narayana Rao was a native of Nashik and the proprietor of the hotel Anand Ashram. Once a scorpion bit his friend. The pain was unbearable. Narayana Rao searched for Baba's *udi,* but could not find it. Immediately he went to Baba's photo, prayed to him and took some ash fallen from the incense sticks. He applied it on the place where the scorpion had bitten his friend and they were surprised when the pain subsided.

The daughter of one of Baba's devotees and the resident of Bandra went to another village where she was struck by plague. The devotee sent word to Nana Chandorkar to send him Baba's *udi.* Word reached Nana at the Thana railway station, as he was on his way with his wife to Kalyan. He did not have Baba's *udi* with him. He did not know what to do. He prayed to Sai, "Baba, I am not in a position to send your *udi* to the devotee who asked for it in full belief. You are all powerful. By repeating your sacred name, I will pick a little of this earth and thinking that I am giving this to the girl in the village, I will apply it on the forehead of my wife. Kindly save the girl from plague fever." The person who came to take *udi* from Nana watched all that took place. When he went back to the village he was surprised to find that the fever had subsided almost at the same time as when Nana Chandorkar had put the earth on the forehead of his wife, invoking the name of Baba.

The nephew of a doctor who lived in Malegaon suffered from an incurable disease, tubercular bone-abcess. A number of medicines were used, without any result. So his parents brought him to Shirdi. Baba asked them to put *udi* on the abcess and it would get cured in a week's time, adding, "This is not a mosque. It is Dwarakamai. Whoever places his foot in it will have good health and happiness. All their difficulties will be over." So saying, Baba slowly massaged the abcess with his hand. He glanced at the boy with compassion. The pain began to subside after the application of *udi* and the abcess was cured completely in due course.

Once Shama's brother's wife had an attack of plague. She had two bubos in her groins. Shama's brother requested him to seek the help of Baba. Then it was night time. Shama went running to Baba and told him about this. Baba told him, "Do not night time. You send *udi* and there is nothing to fear. For all of us the father and head is only that God—*Sab ka Malik ek hai.* You can go tomorrow morning and return quickly." The *udi* was sent through Shama's brother. When Shama went to his brother's house the next morning he found his sister-in-law completely recovered and personally preparing tea. He recollected Baba's advice asking him to go the next morning and realised the significance of Baba's words and was overjoyed.

Dr. Pillay was an intimate devotee of Baba. He often used to sit near Baba and Baba who loved him used to discuss many matters with him. The doctor was once suffering from guineaworms and the pain became unbearable. He went to Kaka Dixit and told him that he could not withstand the pain anymore and preferred death. He requested Kaka to go to Baba and plead on his behalf to reduce the pain and distribute this suffering over ten births. Kaka Dixit went to Baba and told him about the condition of Dr. Pillay and his request. Baba was moved at this and with compassion told him, "Why should he suffer for ten births. Let him not fear. I can destroy the sins committed by him in the previous birth in ten days' time. I am sitting here in Dwarakamai to give happiness to my devotees in this world as well as the other world. Then why should my devotee desire to die ? Bring Pillay here. I will remove his pain permanently." Pillay was brought to Dwarakamai. Baba gave him his bolster and asked him to take rest. He slowly massaged the abcess and blessed him with his raised hand. He told Pillay that the real remedy was to suffer for the sins of the previous birth and get salvation. "Our own actions are responsible for our sorrows and pleasures. Have patience, Allah can only remove the sorrows. If you meditate on God, he will look after you. You have to give him your all—body, mind, wealth and surrender yourself completely. Then God will definitely protect us. God is the head of all of us, Allah Malik. Just now a crow will come and peck you on the abcess and then you will get cured."

In the meanwhile, a boy named Abdul came and started cleaning the lights in the mosque. His leg accidentally touched the abcess and seven guineaworms came out of the abcess. Afterwards, due to applying *udi* on the abcess, there was complete cure in ten days without using any medicines.

Baba's, *udi* completely cured the fits of the daughter of an Iranian devotee; cured the old man from Hardha of a stone in the kidney; corrected the obstruction at the time of delivery experienced each time by a Bombay lady.

Whenever a gentleman of Bandra, tried to sleep, his departed father appeared in his dream and abused and scolded him severely with the result that he could not sleep. He had been suffering from insomnia thus for a long time. His friend advised him to take a little of Baba's *udi* inside and also put it on his forehead before going to sleep every night. After doing this he could sleep peacefully. This gentleman became a Sai devotee and putting up a photo of Sai in his house started worshipping it.

Kaka Mahajani's friend was against idol worship. He went to Shirdi once to witness the miracles and *leelas* of Sai Baba. Before going to Shirdi he told Kaka Mahajan that he would not give *dakshina* to Baba or prostrate before him. When they reached Shirdi, Baba welcomed Kaka Mahajan's friend with pleasing words. The voice with which Baba spoke resembled that of his departed father. For just a moment Baba appeared to him as his father. His joy knew no bounds. He went up the stairs of the mosque saying it was really his father and so saying fell at the feet of Baba and wept. When he got up after in a few minutes, he found Baba and not his father. Then Baba said to him "You did not like to give *dakshina.* So I did not ask you. Remove the screen between us. Then we can see each other clearly, and be happy. We are not different from each other. I am in you and you are in me. At least in future, do not have that differentiation." So saying Baba ordered him to go back to his house early. Without any obstacles in the way he reached home safely. He recollected Baba's words frequently and derived a lot of happiness. As soon as he opened the door, a sparrow flew out fast. He found two dead sparrows inside. He might have locked the door while going to Shirdi without noticing the three sparrows inside the house. Even though two sparrows died, to save the third sparrow Baba might have ordered him to go home immediately. Realising this he was surprised at Baba's love towards all living things.

Some looked at Baba with a critical eye. So many divisions and sub-divisions in Hindu religion made the common man think wonder if there was God at all. Besides, with the growth of materialism, God's devotees were depicted as worthless in cinemas and modern literature. This led to the youth mocking at God and His devotees. A high court pleader named Thakkar who had such modern thoughts, owned a company in which Kaka Mahajani worked as a Manager. He considered modern education and intelligence to be more important than devotion to God and was also of the opinion that love towards mankind was more important than an offering made to God. So, with the motive of criticising that Baba was collecting money in the form of *dakshina* and also to find out the truth in his *leelas* and miracles, Thakkar came with Kaka Mahajani to Shirdi during the Holi festival holidays. Kaka bought two seers of dried grapes for offering to Baba. When he presented the grapes to Baba after *darshan,* Baba ordered that the grapes may be distributed to all the devotees present there. Thakkar, not knowing how to dispose of the seeds in the grapes, for throwing them in the mosque was not proper, put them in his pocket. He considered putting the seeds removed from his mouth after chewing the grapes in his pocket to be below his dignity and blamed Baba inside his heart for creating such a situation.

Noticing the thoughts of Thakkar, Baba called him and gave him some more grapes out of the earlier stock brought by Kaka and asked him to eat them. As he did not like to eat them, he kept them in his hand. But Baba again asked him to eat them. When Thakkar ate the grapes this time, there were no seeds in them. He questioned others about the grapes they had eaten and found out that there were no seeds in the grapes. As he had wanted to see some miracles of Baba, he thought Baba had shown him this miracle. Kaka Mahajani introduced Thakkar to Baba as his master. Then

Baba told that Thakkar may be the master of Kaka, but there was another Master for Thakkar who was the Master for all Allah *Malik hai.* So saying he blessed Thakkar, who then fell at the feet of Baba, lost in complete bliss. While he thus prostrated before Baba's feet he found them resembling those of Lord Vishnu. But when he got up, he found Baba's feet only. After witnessing this, Thakkar prostrated with more devotion at Baba's feet for second time and Baba told him, "God is Omnipresent, and Omnipotent; you cannot see God so easily with your five senses and mind. Every person should try to acquire that power to see God. Though service unto mankind is service unto God, one should not forget God."

Baba clarified his doubts regarding *dakshina* saying, "I will take *dakshina* from only those who were indebted to the mother of the mosque. I will take *dakshina* from those pointed out by the mother only. If I take a rupee as *dakshina,* I have to repay ten times of it to them. This is my principle. Those who give offering or charity now are sowing seeds. This will give a good crop in future. If you give to others in this birth, you will get back in your next birth. Detachment will grow with the charities you make and with this, devotion will increase and you will get *Jnana.* You give a charity of one rupee now and get back ten rupees in future."

Offering Everything to Sai

Balaji Patil Navaskar was a resident of Shirdi and a great devotee of Baba. He used to sweep all lanes through which Baba walked. Every year he used to get his entire crop and offer it to Baba, taking home only that much given to him by Baba for the maintenance of his family. Because of the complete confidence reposed in Baba, his family never faced any difficulties. Baba's words, "There won't be any wanting in my devotees' house," proved to be true in the case of Balaji Patil Navaskar and the following was an example of this.

Once when Navaskar invited his relations for dinner, three times the expected number arrived. The family members were worried that the food prepared may not be sufficient for all. Praying to Sai, they covered all the vessels containing the food items with a cloth and put some Sai *udi* over it and without removing the cloth covers completely, they started serving the dinner. After everyone had dinner, there was still some food left over in the vessels. Thus Baba's assurance proved to be true.

The devotees who have read the chapters explaining the greatness of *udi,* should consider the *udi* as a cure for all ailments and keep it always with them. They should take a little of it every morning after washing the in mouth, then sprinkle some on any new thing purchased and then only use it. After taking bath, they may apply it on the forehead.

Om Shanti ! Shanti ! Shantihi !

CHAPTER 16

How Sai saved Sathe from Ruin

Sathe moved close with Baba. But there was not much spiritual progress in him. Though he grew older he could not control his desire for lust.

In Shirdi was a beautiful woman who attracted males desirous of satisfying their lust. Sathe once went to see Baba, before visiting her. On seeing him, Baba asked him whether he is on his way to 'Saala', the place of the ill-repute woman. But Sathe, not aware of this nickname for the place, thought Baba was asking him about school (meaning *saala*) and gave some vague answer. Afterwards he went to the house of the woman and sat in the verandah, indulging in some pleasant talks. The talks appeared to take Sathe on a ruiness path. When he opened the doors of the room, he was shocked to find Baba standing there and staring at him with his sharp eyes, as if to caution Sathe. Baba also made some gestures with his hand which appeared as though he was questioning him whether he had all the way come to Shirdi only to get ruined. He immediately turned back and came to the mosque. He fell at the feet of Baba and took a vow not to visit that woman again during his lifetime. Then Baba blessed him with his hand raised. In this incident Baba did not speak much, but did everything silently. Baba corrected the wrongs of his devotees in such a way that only those who committed them would understand without others knowing about them.

Meghashyam

Meghashyam was a great devotee of Lord Shiva. He regarded Baba as an Avatar of Shiva. When some devotees gave Baba Shiva's idol from Panipat, he presented it to Megha in appreciation of his devotion to Shiva. Megha did *abhishek* to this idol everyday. After some time the idol was put below the neem tree in Gurusthan, which can be seen even now.

One afternoon, Megha was sleeping in his room in Sathe Wada bolting it from inside. Baba appeared to him in his dream and said "Megha! Draw the trident *(trishul)* near the Shivalinga and sprinkled some *akshatas* (rice) on him." When Megha woke up and looked around, he did not find Baba. But he found the *akshatas* sprinkled by Baba all over the room.

Megha went to Dwarakamai and asked Baba whether he had come to Wada and ordered him to draw the trident *(trishul).* Baba replied in the affirmative. Megha then asked him how he entered the room when it was bolted from inside. Baba replied, "Son, do you think that Baba is only the physical body that you are seeing? I am everywhere. Walls and doors cannot obstruct my movements."

Megha died in the year 1912. Baba touched his dead body and declared that he had been a real devotee, and tears fell from his eyes. He entrusted the work connected with cremation and the obsequies of Megha to Kaka Dixit. After a few days, Shama asked Baba when he was alone, "Baba, we are unable to understand your actions. You used to tell us that death is only to the body and not *Atma* which is permanent. But when Megha died you shed tears and also accompanied the body for some distance. Why did you have this special affection for Megha?" At this Baba smiled and said, "Shama! You have put a wise question. The two doubts you are entertaining are true. But it is necessary to understand properly the connection between them. Every issue is connected with the prevailing conditions in this world and also the timing of the actions. Keeping these in mind, one should try to understand the matter. When this is absent, sometimes the Guru will be viewed critically. When the disciple is in a position to criticise his Guru he does not stand to benefit anything from him, but on the other hand misunderstandings may develop. Things which we cannot properly understand, should not be left to our limited knowledge. Every disciple will face such a situation. But those who offer everything to their Guru wholeheartedly, will consider the actions of the Guru for our good only. In such case there will not be room for duality in thoughts and actions.

"In the present issue, it is a fact that *Atma* is permanent and the body only dies. Usually those who die are born again with some other body. But Megha had completely detached himself from all worldy things. He attained *moksha* (salvation). In the shape of *Atma* he is going far beyond the sun and the moon. That is the reason why I grieved about him."

Mhalsapathi, hearing these clarifications by Baba, was pleased and satisfied with them. Baba looked at Mhalsapathi and said, "Bhagat! One who does not seek answer to his doubts will remain ignorant. But one who seeks answer will be ignorant only till he asks and after that he will be a learned person."

Baba Sanctifying the Religious books

Some devotees of Baba, before reading the religious books gave them to Baba. Baba opened the books, looked into some pages and returned them to the devotees. The devotees believed that by reading those books touched by Baba, they would properly understand the contents, and the *Parayana* would continue unhindered.

Once Kaka Mahajani brought the book *Eknath Bhagwat* to Shirdi. Shama came to the mosque with this book, wanting to read it. Baba took the book from Shama, touched it and returned it to him, asking him to keep it with him only. But Shama told him that the book belonged to Kaka and therefore should be returned to him. But Baba replied, "I am giving this book to you." In this way Baba gave several books to Shama. Shama was an innocent person with a blind devotion. He had no education, and had not read many religious books. Hence Baba gave him a number of religious books.

Once a devotee Ramdas came to Shirdi. He was a great devotee of Lord Rama. He stayed at Shirdi for some days. Every day sitting in the front side of the mosque, he read *Vishnu Sahasranamam* and *Aadyatmika Ramayana.* He made this *Parayan* several times. One day, while he was reading the *Vishnu Sahasranamam,* Baba sent him out on an errand. He obeyed Baba and stopped the *Parayan* in the middle. After Ramdas left, Baba took the *Vishnu Sahasranamam* book of Ramdas and gave it to Shama, saying, "Shama, this *Vishnu Sahasranamam* book is very valuable, which gives good results. I am presenting this to you. You read this sincerely with devotion. Once when my heart was beating rapidly, I suffered a lot and thought that my life was in danger. Under such difficult conditions, I put this book on my heart. It did a lot good and the suffering reduced. I thought Allah had come personally and cured my ailment. I am giving such a powerful book to you. If you read daily one *Namam* also, a lot of good will happen to you."

But Shama hesitated to take the book as it belonged to Ramdas, who was an angry and quarrelsome person and a quarrel might take place when Ramdas returned. But he failed to understand that Baba's aim was to do him good. On his return Ramdas learnt about this and created a scene even though Shama narrated the facts. Then Baba called Ramdas and said to him, "Ramdas, why are you in an angry and quarrelsome mood? Shama had nothing to do in the matter. I gave the book him. Is he not our man? Why are you quarreling with him unnecessarily? Always talk softly and with love. Even though you reading sacred religious books daily, your mind still is not purified. A real Rama *bhakta* should practise equality and detachment and not attachment. With money you can purchase any number of books but not persons. Think well and act intelligently. You know this book 'by heart'. Let Shama also read this and be benefited. If you desire, you can have some other book from Shama in exchange for your book."

Hearing this loving advice from Baba, Ramdas cooled down and took the book *Pancharatna Gita* from Shama, in exchange for his book. The above speech of Baba was not only intended for Ramdas but to all of us. Even though we read a lot of religious books or spend our time in the worship of God, there will not be any benefit unless our hearts get purified.

Attachments to outside things, and the words 'I' and 'mine' should be rid of from us. We must always think that all are one and equal. Everyone should try for such a change of hearts.

Once Bapu Saheb Jog took the *Gita Rahasyam (Secrets of Bhagavad Gita)* written by Tilak, along with him to Baba's *darshan.* Baba took the book from Jog and after seeing some of the inside pages, he took out a rupee coin from his pocket and returned the book to Jog along with the *dakshina,* and blessed him saying that a lot of good would come to him if he read the book sincerely with devotion.

In the same way as Baba used to touch the religious books and bless his devotees, even now when the devotees purchase the books they keep them on the Samadhi of Baba and only then commence the *Parayana.* The same is also in the case when new articles are purchased by the devotees.

Saiyuga

Shirdi Sai Baba was the human incarnation of Lord Shiva of Kailash. For the good of the world, he stopped the poison in his throat and suffered for the sake of others. Repeating the name of such a Sai makes us happy. Worship of Sai is auspicious. Devotees experienced complete bliss when they were in the company of Sai. Baba frequently said, "Allah

Malik". Sai, without aspiring for *moksha* or complete merger in God, had remained in the service of all living beings considered by him as facets of God. Sai means love, selfless love, sacred love. Sai's love was not only to mankind but all living things. People in the name of wealth, caste, religion, nationality, regions and political parties swindle and become millionaires. If necessary they are prepared to kill some. In the present society we find a lot of such persons who call themselves leaders and servants of people. To curb this we should publicise Sai philosophy on a large scale, spreading brotherly love in society. All should have peace and happiness permanently. This shall be the aim of *Sai Prachar*. That is why you find an awakening to Sai philosophy in all nooks and corners of our towns and villages of the country. *Sai Yuga* is going to set in. All castes, all religions and all philosophies will merge into one and the philosophy of 'One family' will be established and we be lucky to be a part of this movement. Let us pray to Sai Baba to form an army of dedicated devotees (Sai Army) and establish a Sai empire.

Om Shanti ! Shanti ! Shantihi !

Chapter 17

God sends *yogis* to different places in this world to propagate spiritual matters to counter the growing evils and balance this to a certain extent. This is the main aim of the *yogis* or religious leaders. Though they function at different places, they know each other and from where they are functioning. As Vasu Devananda Saraswathi said, Shirdi Sai Baba was like an elder brother to all such *yogis*.

We come in contact with *yogis* because of our good actions of the previous birth. Persons who did no good in their previous births, will fall prey to desires and lead the lives of animals as they cannot put their minds to divine ways. Because of the good actions in our previous birth, today we are lucky to do *Parayana* of the *Life History of Shirdi Sai Baba,* who is the king of all *yogis*.

Appa—The Kannada Yogi

Thakur was working as a clerk in the Revenue Department. Once he visited the Kannadiga *yogi* Appa and touched his feet in reverence. Appa gave him a book on Vedanta titled *Vichara Sagara,* and asked him to read it without fail as this would fulfil his wishes. He said, "Sometime in the future when you go in the northerly direction on official work, you would be lucky to come in contact with a great *yogi*. By his *darshan* you will have peace of mind and happiness. He will show you the proper way to your life's journey." After sometime Thakur was transferred to a place called Jinner. To reach it he had to cross a deep valley by riding on a buffalo. He suffered a lot while he was at Jinner. After sometime he was transferred on promotion to Kalyan. There he learnt about Baba and his greatness through Nana Chandorkar. He came to Shirdi and by touching Baba's feet he experienced a lot of happiness. Baba who is omnipresent told Thakur, "The road here is not as easy as what Appa told you. It is also not as easy as travelling on a buffalo in the valley. One should work hard relentlessly. Walking on this road is like walking on a sharp-edged sword.

Without asking Thakur who he was, from where he had come and the purpose of his visit, Sai Bhagwan knew everything. After hearing Sai, Thakur's eyes were full of tears out of joy and he experienced complete bliss. He found that what the Kannadiga *yogi* Appa had said was true. With complete devotion he prostrated at the feet of Baba. After putting his hand on 'Thakur's head in an act of blessing, Baba told him, "What Appa had told you is true. But you have to learn them and put them into practice. No useful purpose will be served by simply reading the holy books. The knowledge obtained from the books without the blessings of Guru will be of no use." Every word that came out of Baba was like nectar. The readers should not only take this nectar but also continue on their life's journey in a peaceful manner.

The Nine Forms of Devotion

Ananta Rao Patankar of Poona was a Vedic scholar. Though he read all the *Vedas, Upanishads* and the eighteen *Puranas* he had no peace of mind. He came to Shirdi and visited Baba. On seeing him he experienced a lot of happiness which he did not experienced in his life till then. He fell at Baba's feet and pleaded with him to show compassion and bless him. Then Baba said, "Once a merchant came to me. He wanted to put some questions to me but could not do so. He was looking straight at me. Just then a mare in front of him passed stools in the shape of nine balls. The merchant collected all the nine balls and put them in his upper cloth by which he was able to concentrate his mind and thus have peace." But the scholar Patankar did not understand the analogy between peace of mind and the nine balls. A devotee, Dada Kelkar, at the instigation of Baba, explained the significance of the story as follows.

"Merchant means a person having special qualities not found in ordinary people, a *Jnani.* A mare means God's Grace. Nine balls of horse's excretion means nine kinds of devotion. The devotee in search of God should fix his mind on the Sadguru, and serve the Guru sincerely. Then God will pity him and show him the nine devotional ways. The devotee can choose any one of the nine ways and reach God. The nine ways are:

1.	Shravan	Hearing divine stories and reading the *Puranas.*
2.	Kirtan	Singing devotional songs in praise of the greatness of God.
3.	Smaran	To recollect what one had heard through Shravan, and - always remembering them.
4.	Pada Seva	Worship of the feet and prostration.
5.	Archana	Different kinds of rituals performed daily.
6.	Namaskar	Bowing the head in respect, and salutation.
7.	Dasya	Doing service to God like a servant.
8.	Sakhyatva	Considering God as a friend and making friendship.
9.	Atma Nivedan	Surrendering one's life and *Atma* to God.

Devotion is of nine kinds. As we progress and the mind begins to settle down, we can worship God in all the nine ways. Let us make sincere efforts to reach God through the nine devotional ways like the *Jnani* in the story.

The Story of Avasthe

P.R. Avasthe was a judge at Gwalior. Hearing of the greatness of Baba through Rege, he wanted to see him. In

1914, on his way to Phandaripur, he came to Shirdi along with Rege. Those were the days of the First World War. These two were travelling by train from Gwalior to Manmad. When the train reached Mhow where there were a large number of troops, all the passengers in the train were asked to alight so as to enable the transport of the troops. Avasthe and Rege also had to get off the train. They prayed to Baba to help them. In the meantime the Military Commander came and after inspecting their carriage told them that this was too small to accommodate the troops and told them that they need not get down. The whole night Avasthe sang devotional songs and prayed to Baba. They reached Shirdi the next day morning. When they went to the mosque to see Baba, he asked Rege who the unstable devil with him was. He said, "They tried to disembark my children from the train. But I told the captain that you are my children and let them come to me. But this Avasthe was by my side the whole night, calling 'Baba! Baba!' "

From the above incidents we learn that Baba always protects the devotees who fully believe in him. Previously Avasthe had a *yogini* as his Guru. He thought that now if he started worshipping and serving Baba, he might be considered as unfaithful to the *yogini* who his Guru. But Rege told him that his Guru was also integrated in Sai Baba who is considered to be the incarnation of God and Guru for the entire world (Jagatguru). Hence if he worshipped Sai Baba it amounts to worshipping his Guru *yogini.* But Avashthe desired to have some proof of this. For the afternoon *arathi,* he took a rice ball kept in a small vessel covered with a cloth. He thought within himself that if Baba personally asked and took the rice ball, then he would definitely believe that his Guru *yogini* was also in Baba. He started climbing the steps of Dwarakamai when the rice-ball fell down accidentally. What he had wanted to keep as a secret, became public. When he was picking up the rice ball from the floor, Baba called him and asked him to give it to him and said that he in turn would send it to the person for whom it was intended. Avasthe felt very happy. His Guru *yogini* had attained *Samadhi* long back. He decided to have Baba as his his Guru. Even afterwards Avasthe used to come to Shirdi and consult Baba whenever he wanted advise in worldly matters; spiritually also he advanced much by seeking Sai's advise.

Accepting Sai Baba as Guru

From the above story, the moral we learn is—If the devotees of Sai have had some other Gurus previously, and so think that they are being unfaithful to them, if they treat Sai Baba as their Guru now, no such doubt need be entertained by them, since Sai Baba is the Guru of Gurus, Samartha Sadguru King of Gurus and *yogis.* He has powers to command the entire world and also to control the five elements. If any disciple of a Guru comes under protection of Sai, the Guru will be pleased. Some Gurus with an eye on the wealth and power of their disciples, will try to create some unpleasant situations with some concocted stories.

Baba also was not for changing Gurus. He always checked to see what type of disciple he was and under what circumstances he had left his previous Guru and come to him. There are a number of disciples who would worship a particular Guru or God for some time and if they did not gain anything, they would change their Gurus or Gods. They would run to the Guru or God who fulfilled their wishes. Such persons are after material benefits and not spiritual advancement, being without faith and patience. When they came to Baba, he would tell them, "What is required for you is not another Guru. If you cannot have undeterred devotion and gratitude towards your Guru, but come to me, no useful purpose will be served and you cannot benefit anything. Therefore, first of all you should learn how to serve your own Guru in the correct manner and do not keep changing your Guru." To those who approached Shirdi Sai Baba and saw his greatness personally, and were unable to surrender themselves completely, our appeal to them: "Previously there was no Guru equal to Sai Baba. In future also we cannot get such a Guru. Let us prostrate to this Satchidananda Samartha Sadguru, and request him to make us understand his true Avatar, before we complete the *Parayana* of his *Life History.* We will also pray to him to see that we have abundant devotion for him with this devotion lasting our lifetime. When the life goes out of our body our kith and kin and material things do not come with us. We also pray to Sai to be with us in our solitary journey and to give us *moksha* or higher form of life in the next birth and be with us in all the future births.

Om Shanti ! Shanti ! Shantihi !

CHAPTER 18

The Story of Two Goats

That was the month of May in the year 1909. Geographically situated at a higher altitude, Shirdi had acute shortage of water during summer months. The severe summer made the people very uneasy. In the nights the villagers slept outside in the open though there was no breeze. But in the early hours there was a cool breeze which the villagers enjoyed very much, thinking it to be God-sent. The morning climate was pleasant like the innocent smile of babies laughing.

Baba was going from Dwarakamai towards Lendi Bagh. Behind him were Shama, Tatya, Balashimpi, Bhagoji Shinde and others.

Just then a herd of goats passed that way. Baba caught hold of two goats from the herd. Bhagoji Shinde went to assist Baba. He talked with the owner of the herd and purchased the two goats for Rs. 32. The actual cost of the two goats would not be more than Rs. 7. Baba ordered for five seers of *chana dal* (Bengal gram) and fed the goats. Seeing this strange behaviour of Baba, Shama questioned him about this. Baba replied, "I have neither a house nor family and therefore I should not accumulate wealth." Even then Tatya and Shama were discussing seriously among themselves about the transaction. Baba gave away the two goats to the owner of the herd. Baba explained his strange actions and also the story of the two goats, to the devotees thus; "These two goats were humans in their previous births. They were with me for some time. They were brothers born to the same mother and were effectionate in the beginning. As they grew up, enmity grew between them. The younger brother earned a lot of money with his intelligence. The elder brother, out of jealousy, tried to kill his brother and steal all his money. In this way the two brothers tried to kill each other. At last both of them died at the same place and time by killing each other. Because of their actions in the previous birth, now they are born as goats. When they were passing by me, I recognised them and drew them near to me. From the happy human life they have come down to animal life in this birth and are suffering. In view of their connection with me in their previous births, I wanted to keep them with me and make their lives happy. But you all made a fuss about my transaction and so I returned them to their owner."

From the above-mentioned story of the two goats we learn two things. If we indulge in enmity and quarrels, we will come down from human life to animal life in our next birth. Though the goats were with him in the previous birth, Baba could not keep them with him because his present collegues started murmuring. We must always do things which are liked by all around us, and not hurt the feelings of those who are with us.

Hari Kanoba

A resident of Bombay, Hari Kanoba, on hearing the greatness of Baba came to Shirdi to test the greatness of him. When he went to the mosque he put on his best dress, wore new footwear and sprayed scent on his dress. He did not know where to keep his costly footwear before entering the mosque. He kept them in a corner near the mosque and went in. He waited till his turn came and greeted Baba with folded hands. Baba gave him *udi* as *prasad.* All the while he was in the mosque, his mind was on the new footwear left outside and not on Baba. When he came out of the mosque, he was shocked to find his new footwear missing. Then he began thinking—on hearing of Baba's greatness he had come, but lost his footwear and blamed Baba for what had happened. He went to his room. While he was eating a boy with a stick, at the end of which the footwear was tied, was announcing loudly "Hari Ka Beta, Zari Ka Peta", meaning son of Hari and sporting *zari* headgear. Kanoba came out of his room on hearing the announcement and found his new footwear on the stick carried by the boy. He called the boy and on enquiry he was told that Sai Baba had given him the footwear and asked him to go round the place announcing as stated and if someone responded to this, then to give the footwear to him.

Kanoba then went inside the room and brought and showed the *zari* headgear to the boy, and claiming the footwear, felt immensely happy. He though that Baba might have known his name and about the *zari* headgear. But how could be know about his father's name? Thus Kanoba who had come to test Baba, found him to be of all pervasive.

Fakir Maddhu Shah

In the year 1913, Maddhu Shah, a resident of Meerin village near Jalgaon, came to Shirdi and requested Baba for Rs. 700 which was urgently required for a good cause. At the instance of Baba, Jog gave Rs. 700 in coins to two youths, Lakshman and Gulab with a direction to give this money to Maddhu Shah. But the youths gave only Rs. 500 to the *fakir*, Maddhu Shah, and kept for themselves the balance of Rs. 200.

Maddhu Shah told Baba that he received only Rs. 500. Baba appearing not to have taken note of it, gave the *fakir udi* as *prasad* and sent him away. The *fakir* travelled for about two miles and was near Neemgaon, when a *tahsildar* named Erun Shah, passed in a *tonga*. On seeing the *fakir*, he got down from the *tonga*, gave the food packet he was carrying and also Rs. 200. The *fakir* took the money and food packet, and feeling very happy, continued his journey after some rest.

Erun Shah, the *tahsildar,* reached Shirdi and stayed in the house of Tatya Patil. He told him about a dream he had. In his dream someone told him, "Come to Shirdi in a *tonga.* On your way near Neemgaon you will find a *fakir* with a tiger skin on him. Give him Rs. 200 and also some food." He finding such a *fakir* near Neemgaon he gave him Rs. 200 and some food.

Six months after the above mentioned incident, the two youths, Lakshman and Gulab, came to Erun Shah and gave him Rs. 1,000 each in some other connection. That day again Erun Shah had a dream. Someone told him in his dream, "In your dream about six months back, as per my direction you gave to a *fakir* Rs. 200. Today, I am giving you ten times that." What moral we learn from this story is, Baba collected ten times the amount from Lakshman and Gulab, which they had misappropriated, not caring for Baba's instructions and made the two youths pay to Erun Shah, who obeyed Baba's instructions, ten times the money he had paid to the *fakir.* Those who steal God's money will have to pay back ten times that during this birth or in the future. Under any circumstances one should be willing to spend for God but if one is tempted to take God's money then one will have to suffer.

Desiring Mantropadesa from Baba

An old woman called Radha Bai Deshmukh treated Baba as her Guru and she wanted to have *Mantropadesa* and also *Atma Sakshatkara.* With this determined desire, she went to Shirdi and requested Baba to teach her *mantras.* But Baba kept silent. Then she went on a fast and decided not to take food or water till Baba taught her *mantras.* Her fast continued for three days and she became very weak. Shama noticed this and fearing that Baba might get a bad name if anything happened to her, requested Baba to interfere in the matter and save the woman.

Then Baba sent for her and told, "Mother, I am like your child. You are like my mother. Why are you undergoing this agony and desiring death? I am a *fakir.* Show kindness to me. My Guru was a great 'Satpurusha'. When I approached him, he asked me two coins as *dakshina.* They are not ordinary coins. One is *shraddha* (faith) and the other is *saburi* (patience). *Shraddha* means faith, doing work correctly, and *saburi* means patience — equanimity in the face of difficulties. As soon as he asked for them, I improved these two qualities in me and gave them to my Guru as *dakshina.* He immediately got my head tonsured and accepted my dakshina.

"When my Guru was in meditation I used to sit in front of him, and focus my eyes on his face, without diverting it on other matters; this went on for days, forgetting hunger and thirst. He also used to look at me with love. On such occasions we used to be full of mutual love and happiness. I could not withstand our separation even for a moment. There was no other goal for me except my Guru. I never craved for anything other than my Guru. He also desired to have my love only and nothing else. He used to radiate his affection on me always.

"I will never tell a lie sitting in this mosque. My Guru did not tell me any *mantra* in my ear. So I cannot also give any advice to you. If you want to have me as your Guru, you must behave as I did in the case of my Guru. Keep me as the goal for your thoughts and ideals. See me with undeterred sincerity and I will also see you in the same manner. Some drawbacks and pressures in life will try to separate us. Without yielding to such things you should exercise patience and be happy. Unless you act like this, you cannot reach your life's goal. You need not bother about the four kinds of practices, six *shastras* or eight kinds of yoga. With strong devotion, if you serve your Guru that is enough. This is the only true thing that my Guru taught me."

These nectar-like words of Baba changed the heart of the old woman and she gave up the fast. That day Baba made her sit next to him and eat her food.

Sai's philosophy is above *mantras, pujas* and procedures coming down from ages, and also the blind beliefs. What are required to be given to Sai Baba are our heart, mind and ego. When we offer these three to our Guru, then the five senses will lose their power. A person who controls the five senses will be deemed to have won this world. As advised by Baba, if we focus our eyes on the Guru, some changes will take place in our body. Let us see what these changes are. All our senses will desire external pleasures. This is the natural tendency of the senses. But if we concentrate our mind on the Guru, then the mind will not stray. Then the desires will disappear and the mind will be focussed on Guru only. In the olden days they did penance to achieve this only. If we concentrate our mind on Guru keeping this as our life's aim, then this is equivalent to penance.

Ekalavya could learn and master the arts of warfare, by concentration of his mind and meditation on Dronacharya. Baba's teaching about devotion to Guru is also like penance. Keep these in mind and read the words of Baba once more. In these days, where weaker sections of our society cannot do sacrificial rites, Sai who descended from Kailash has shown this easy way to attain *moksha.* Wishing all the readers will go in the Sai Marga and enjoy peace and happiness.

Om Shanti ! Shanti ! Shantihi !

End of Third Day's Parayana

FOURTH DAY'S 'PARAYANA'—SUNDAY

CHAPTER 19

Das Ganu resigned his job in the year 1903, and completely devoted himself to Sai and fully immersed in spreading Baba's philosophy. All worldly desires left him. Through *Hari Kathas* and *kirtans* he began explaining the spiritual matters to others. Because of this he could also easily learn with Baba's Grace, many matters relating to *Bhakti, Jnana* and *Vairagya.* If we keep our mind stable and peaceful, *Jnana* comes by itself with Guru's blessings. With *Jnana* obtained in such a manner, Das Ganu wrote and published *Shanta Kathamrutham* in the year 1905 and *Bhakta Leelamrutam* in the year 1906. Hemad Pant started writing Baba's life history in the year 1917 and finished it in the year 1929. Till this became available to devotees, they used to read the above-mentioned two books of Das Ganu. There are a number of Sai *leelas* in these two books.

Nanavali

A number of devotees used to approach Baba with materialistic desires. Nanavali used to observe all this from a distance. He used to put only an upper cloth on him and looked like a mentally deranged person. His talk was harsh and eyes fearful to look at, usually no one talked to him. He never tolerated any injustice and if he came across such a thing he went there and condemned it with his harsh words. The public moved away if they noticed him coming. If he came across any persons having bad ideas or thoughts, he scolded them with harsh words and sometimes threw stones at them.

He never tolerated it if anyone talked against Baba. Such was his devotion towards Baba. One day he noticed some merchants asking Baba about money matters and troubling him much. He came forward quickly and sat in front of Baba, demanding, "*Fakir*! I want a big tree which bears money immediately. I do not want a small tree which cannot give me money just now. It should give money the moment it sprouts." Baba cooled the temper of Nanavali and assured him that he would grant his request and Nanavali went away laughing.

The devotees present there conveyed their feeling to Baba that it was not good for Baba to entertain Nanavali, who was a crazy person. Baba replied as follows, "While I am sitting in this mosque to show you *Jnana Marga* leading to salvation, you are coming to me for wealth, fame, status and other materialistic desires. What is it that one has to achieve in his lifetime? Is wealth the only thing? No, but wealth is also necessary—only up to the level of leading a normal life and that too with money earned the right way. Even if you earn and accumulate a lot of wealth out of greed, throughout your life, it is a fact that nothing will come with you after you die.

"My spiritual treasury is overflowing. I can give whatever devotees desire. They can also come and take away whatever amount they like. But they should qualify themselves for receiving it. But they are not willing to take what I give them, they want only what they desire. I am prepared to give them priceless gold. But they choose only earthen lumps.

"From where did we come into this human body? What we are doing now? From here, where are we going ? Who is behind our births and deaths ? Who created the sun, the moon, the stars and other planets ? People don't think about all this. They are only after wealth and physical happiness, thinking that this life is permanent. But they are getting destroyed like the insects which, drawn to the flame perish. This is complete *Agnana* (ignorana) which is quiet opposite to *Jnana Marga*. I came in this body only to put humanity in the *Jnana Marga*.

Many a time Baba elaborated the word "I and Me" through his teachings. To know about me or to search for me you need not go elsewhere. If you remove your name and form, then what is left in you is myself. Not only in you but I am equally present in all living beings. If you realise this, then you can see me in all living things. If you cause any pain to any living thing, you are hurting me. Those who tolerate the hardships caused to them by others, are dear to me."

Chandra Bai Borkar

Chandra Bai Borkar visited Shirdi for the first time in the year 1898 at the age of 28. The mud walls of the mosque (Dwārakamai) were in a bad condition. In those days Baba used to spend most of his time sitting under the neem tree. Chandra had personally seen Baba lighting the lamps with water. She had also seen Baba sleeping on the narrow wooden board tied to the rafters of the mosque with lengths of cloth pieces and with lamps on the four corners of the board.

Her husband was Ramachandra Borkar, an engineer. In 1909, he was supervising the construction of a bridge near Pandarpur. During that period, she came to Shirdi and spent many days in the presence of Baba. But Ramachandra Borkar never visited Shirdi. One day, Baba called her and told, "Mother, go to Phandarpur. I will also come along with you." She went with two other ladies to Pandarpur and found that her husband had left the place a short while before her arrival. So again she set out to Shirdi. But the money amongst all the three was just sufficient to purchase tickets only up to Khurudwadi station. At Khurudwadi a *fakir* came to them and told her that her husband was at Dhond railway station and asked them to go there. But she had no money to go there. When she told him this he immediately put three tickets for Dhond Station in her hand and left the place. The ladies left for Dhond.

Ramachander Borkar was sitting on the platform of Dhond railway station, half asleep. A *fakir* appeared before him and asked him how he forgot his wife, saying that his wife would be coming shortly by train to Dhond. He gave him a slip with the number of the rail coach in which she is coming. Ramachander Borkar came out of his sleepy state and found a slip in his hand and concluded it was not a dream. Just then a train arrived on the platform and he saw his wife coming out of the coach. He immediately told her of the miracle that had happened. Then she also told him what all had happened. Having experienced Baba's nectar like love for them, they felt immensely happy. Chandra Bai Borkar's story is one of such several instances when several couples who got separated for one reason or other got united again by praying to Baba.

In 1910-11, our country was under the rule of the British. Those were the days when the Indian National Congress under the presidentship of Dadabhai Naoroji resolved to have self-rule for our country. Among the then Congress leaders, there were extremists who believed in achieving their object by violent methods and those who believed in non-violent methods. Bal Gangadhar Tilak was the leader of the extremists and coined the slogan "Freedom is my Birthright", demanding complete freedom to our country immediately, touring in all directions of the country, giving lectures and awakening the masses. The British government arrested them under 'Sedition' and sent them to jails outside India. B.G. Tilak was sent to a jail in Mandalay in Burma. A close associate of Tilak was Diwan Bahadur Ganesh Sri Krishna Khaparde. Being the right hand person to Tilak he feared his arrest. Deciding that except Shirdi Sai Baba none can save him, he came to Shirdi on 5 December 1910 and served Baba.

G.S. Khaparde

G. S. Khaparde was a leading advocate of Amroti, earned a lot. Having associated in the freedom movement he came in contact with several people. He was very much interested in name and fame, wealth and family happiness. On the day of his arrival at Shirdi, Baba told him, "This is your house. You can stay here fearlessly. When I am here as your protector, you need not fear anything." These words of Baba coincided with his thoughts.

After staying at Shirdi for a week, Khaparde went back to Amroti. He came for the second time to Shirdi along with his family on 6 December 1911 and approached Sai Baba without any reservations, with a pure heart, mind and body. Baba detained him at Shirdi for a period of $3^{1}/_{2}$ months, till his problems were solved.

Kashinath Govind Upasani Shastri (Upasani Baba)

As there was no other way out to remove his bodily ailment, Kashinath came to Shirdi on 27 June 1911. As soon as he entered Dwarakamai, Baba told him "Son I know you for the past seven births. If you stay at Shirdi, you will achieve your goal in life. Because of your good deeds in your previous birth, you achieved spiritual progress. If you stay here for some time with a stable mind you will reach a higher state." So saying Baba blessed him. When Kashinath approached Baba on the third day for permission to leave Shirdi, Baba declined to permit him and asked him to stay at Shirdi. "In case you want to go, come back in a week's time."

Kashinath left Shirdi and several strange things happened even before he reached home. He returned to Shirdi on the seventh day, as advised by Baba. Before he reached Shirdi, Baba appeared to him in several forms and gave him some indications. Baba made him recollect these things and ordered him to stay for 4 years at Khandoba temple, meditating.

During the period Baba taught Upasini several matters and showed several *leelas* and experiences. These methods on teaching were very strange and beyond our imagination. We cannot find similar things anywhere in the sacred books. The divine powers in Kashinath went on increasing with the increased period of his meditation. The testing by Baba increased along with the increase in Upasani's divine powers. Seeing the powers of Upasani, some Sai devotees approached him and invited him to their places. But he should not go out during the period of *diksha.* On the other hand he could not withstand to the tests put by Baba. At last without completing the four year period prescribed by Baba, he left Shirdi secretly in the night without informing Baba on 25 July 1914, a few months earlier. We also may sometimes be unable to withstand the *Maya* and be distanced from Baba. Let all the Sai devotees have complete faith in Baba and treat his word as the word of God. Let their thoughts be on Sai only and none else.

Om Shanti ! Shanti ! Shantihi !

CHAPTER 20

Human life is full of desires, greed and sensory pleasures. Even if we control these things for a long time, we do not know when they will raise their ugly heads. Due the influence of *Maya,* a person one will distance himself from God and lead a lowly life. The path reach God is full of thorns and ditches. Even though a person has learned all the *Vedas,* etc., he cannot go on this path safely. Only he who has already travelled in this path and knows where the ditches are and where the thorns are, can guide us safely to our destination. Such a guide is a 'Guru'.

One day Baba narrated his experience in the form of a story to Shama, Tatya, Noolkar and others, near Gurusthan. It goes as follows.

In Quest of God

Once four of us, thinking we are great learned men, went into the forest. Having heard that there was a temple for the forest deity belonging to the *banjaras* (nomads), we went in search of it. It was a deserted place. While proceeding we were discussing the ways to reach God. One opined that it was enough if we controlled our mind, another expressed that it was enough if we know about *Atma,* and so on. But I told them, "We must perform our duties properly and place our body, mind and the five *pranas* at the feet of the Guru and seek his protection. Then with the blessings of the Guru we can reach God easily." As we were walking a *banjara* who was coming in the opposite direction, asked us where we were going. One gave an indifferent reply to him thinking that it was below his dignity to talk to such a person. The Banjara waited for sometime and offered to accompany us and show us the way to the place of our destination. But we proceeded quickly, ignoring him. We roamed in the forest till evening without finding the temple. Luckily, we came back to the place from where we had set out. Again the same *banjara* was waiting for us. He told that if we had taken his help, we should have definitely seen the temple. "But never mind. You are lucky to have come back to this place. You seem to be very hungry. Please take this food," and offered them food. The others felt insulted and went away. But as I am hungry, I ate the food given by the Banjara and drank water. To my surprise, my Guru appeared in the place of the Banjara. Then I respectfully greeted him with folded hands. My Guru asked me whether I would go with him. I told that I was bound by my Guru's orders.

My Guru took me near a well. He tied my legs together with a rope. Then he tied me upside down to the branch of a tree on the well. He lowered my body in that position into the well until I was two feet above the water. After hanging me like that, my Guru left me. Slowly the place became dark due to nightfall. I heard the tigers roaring from above the well. Inside the well poisonous snakes were hissing. I could not see anything in the pitch darkness. My Guru was very competent. When his protection was there, why should I fear these snakes and tigers? After four or five hours, my Guru came and lifted me up from the well. He asked me how I felt. I told him that I felt very happy. He then asked me whether I had feared at any time. I replied that when he had personally brought me there, why I should fear? Then my Guru, patting me on my shoulders with affection, blessed me. His love for me was more than that of a mother. He admitted me in his *Gurukul* (school). His love made me forget my parents. I used to look at him with concentration. Every word coming out of him was equal to that of God's. My house, my property and my parents, all are my Guru only. All my sensory organs left their places and lay centred near my eyes. My eyes were always fixed on my Guru. Except for this I was conscious of nothing else.

With the blessings of my Guru and without any effort, *Atma Jnana* came to me. I could understand everything in this creation, just like daylight. This is the effect of my Guru on me. The right conduct, wealth, and desires can be acquired by humans with their efforts. But 'Moksha' can be achieved only with the help of a competent Guru.

Baba's narration of his personal experience, must have taken place while he was under his Guru Venkusa's care. What we learn from this story is that we must have the help of a Guru, when in quest of God. Without going to a Guru and reposing full faith in him, we cannot know God.

Obeying Baba's Orders

For the people of Shirdi, Baba was the incarnation of God. When the devotees took leave of Baba, he gave certain suggestions. The devotees took them as Baba's orders and followed them strictly. If a person not follow Baba's suggestion, he met with some difficulty.

Once Tatya Kote Patil was on his way to the shandy at Kopargaon in a tonga. He went to see Baba, who advised him not to leave Shirdi. But Tatya replied that when Baba was there, he had no fear and continued his journey. After going some distance, one of the legs of the horse got sprained and the horse sank on its legs, and the tonga fell down. There was no serious danger, but Tatya had to come back to Shirdi. Tatya was grateful to Baba for his motherly love and for foreseeing the mishap and advising him not to go.

A doctor from Europe once came to see Baba. He wanted to go inside the mosque and kiss Baba's hand. But Baba did not allow him inside the mosque and asked him to pay his respects from outside. The visitor felt insulted and wanted to leave Shirdi immediately. But Baba advised him to leave the next day. Without heeding Baba's advice, he left Shirdi immediately. After proceeding for some distance, the horse took fright due to some unforeseen reason, and the tonga fell down; the doctor was dragged for some distance, with the result that he received injuries all over the body and had to be hospitalised for several days in a hospital in Kopargaon. What the above two incidents mean are:

i) Though Tatya went against the advise of Baba, he put the burden on, Baba expressing complete faith in him, and he escaped from danger.

ii) The foreigner thought that Baba had insulted him and went away without realising that what Baba had advised him was for his good only.

Even what Tatya had done was also not correct. Disobeying Baba and then putting the burden on Baba was also not proper. It was a foolish act.

Ramchander Atmaram

Ramchander Atmaram belonged to 'Prardhana Samaj'. He was also known as Baba Saheb Tarkhad. Members of the Samaj do not accept idol worship. He was an advocate practising at Bandra. He was a broadminded humanist. But his wife and sons were devotees of Shirdi Sai Baba. His son got up early in the morning daily and after ablutions, worshipped Baba with his photo before him and only then attended to other work.

Once Atmaram's wife wanted to go to Shirdi and have *Darshan* of Baba. Atmaram wanted his son to accompany her. But his son declined stating that if both he and his mother were absent from the house, then there would be none to worship the photo of Baba.

Though Atmaram was against idol worship, he agreed to worship Baba's photo daily in the same way that his son worshipped, till his son and wife returned, and sent them to Shirdi. The first two days Atmaram worshipped Baba's photo properly and had Baba's *prasad* before he took lunch. On the third day, Monday, due to urgent court work, he finished the worship early and went away. When he returned for lunch he wanted to have Baba's *prasad* first. But his cook told him that no *prasad* had been offered to Baba in the morning worship by Atmaram as he had gone out in a hurry and forgotten about offering sugar candy to Baba. On hearing this, Atmaram got up and went to the *puja* room and found the plate empty. He felt guilty and bowed his head before Baba. What his son feared had happened. As a punishment for not offering Baba sugar candy, he decided not to take his lunch and went back to court.

At about the same time, Atmaram's son and wife stood with devotion before Baba in Dwarakamai. Baba called Atmaram's wife and told her that when he went to their house in Bandra that day to eat something, he found the *puja* room locked, but even then he went inside and found nothing there which he could eat and so returned hungry. He further told her that her husband also had not taken food that day for having sent Baba away hungry. She was surprised at Baba's revelation and immediately wrote a letter to Atmarams to Bandra.

That day after going to court again in the afternoon, Atmaram wrote a letter to his son at Shirdi, explaining the lapse on his part. On the third day both the letters reached their destinations. On seeing his father's letter, the son ran to Baba with the letter. Baba told him, "Son, do not fear. In future your father will never forget me. He will also worship my photo as you do. You can stay here as long as you wish."

On reading the letter received from Shirdi, Atmaram wondered how Baba could have know his lapse in forgetting to offer *prasad* and his observing fast as a punishment for this. He came to the conclusion that there was no difference between Baba and his photo and that idol worship was not incorrect if worshipped with faith. From that day onwards he took a vow before Baba's photo that he also would daily do Baba's worship along with his son. He felt very happy with the way things had happened through his son. Usually children learn spiritual matters from parents. But in this case, the son acted as a guide to his father and brought him into Sai's fold. Atmaram was really lucky to have such a son.

All readers, irrespective of age, who are doing *Parayana* of this *Life History of Baba* should understand the moral in each story and try to emulate them in their life. They should stand out as model Sai devotees. Let us also pray to Sai Baba to fulfil his responsibility also by guiding us towards attaining *moksha*.

Om Shanti ! Shanti ! Shantihi !

CHAPTER 21

Sometimes Baba narrated his experiences in the form of a story. One day, after watering the plants in Lendi Bagh Baba was sitting with Tatya under a nearby tree. Then Bhate and other devotees came there and sat with them. Baba shared his reminiscences with them.

Veerabhadrappa—Chenna Basappa

One morning I went for a stroll, and going some distance, I rested under a tree by the side of a rivulet. A traveller came there and sat near me. A frog was croaking. He enquired me about it. I told him that the frog was tasting the bitter fruits of its *karma* (past actions). We have to reap the consequences of our actions whether right or wrong, of the previous birth, in this birth. He went to the spot from where the croaking sound was coming and found a black snake holding a frog in its mouth. I told him that both had been wicked in their previous birth and were reaping the consequences in this birth. He told me that the snake would devour the frog in a few minutes. I told him that I was like a father to the frog and would not allow it to die. Then we both went to the place where the snake was. I went near the snake and addressed it, "What Veerabhadrappa! Your foe Chenna Basappa had taken the form of a frog in this birth and is leading a lowly life. Though you are born as a snake, the enmity between you two has not subsided! Why are you having this enmity? You leave your hatred for each other and cool down."

On hearing my words, the snake released the frog and went into the water. The frog went away hopping. The traveller who was with me was surprised and asked me to tell him about Veerabhadrappa and Chenna Basappa. Then I narrated to him the details of the previous birth of the snake and the frog, as follows.

There was a dilapidated Shiva temple near a village named Mayuri. The villagers collected donations on a large scale, for getting the temple renovated. They appointed a wealthy man of the village as treasurer and handed over the collected amount to him. The person was a miser. He spent only a small amount for the temple but showed huge expenditure in the accounts. There was no improvement of the temple. If anyone questioned him, he put them off by his sweet words.

After some days, the deity in the temple, Mahadev appeared in the dreams of the miser's wife and told her, "Construct the dome of the temple. I will pay back 100 times of the money you spend for this." When she told her husband about the dream, he laughed it off saying that it was only a dream and could be relied upon. When he was there, why did Mahadev tell her, ignoring him? The main aim of the dream appears to be to create ill-feelings between wife and husband. She became helpless and kept quiet.

Again after some days, Mahadev appeared in her dream and told her not to ask from her husband any money but to construct the dome of the temple with her money. She told her husband about this dream and decided to donate her jewels given to her by her parents, for the construction of the dome. Her miserly husband did not like this idea. He underestimated the value of the jewels as rupees one thousand and in exchange, without giving her the amount, gave her some dry land unfit for cultivation. Even this land did not belong to him. A poor old woman named Dubaki had pledged this piece of land with the miser for two hundred rupees and as she could not redeem it, the miser had annexed it. This cunning miser not only deceived his wife and Dubaki but also God. As this land is of no use, it was handed over to the temple priest.

After a period, a big cyclone hit the land and it rained heavily. During this time lightning struck the house of the miser and he and his wife died. In course of time Dubaki also died. In his next birth, the miser was born to a poor brahmin couple in Mathura and named Veerabhadrappa who lived by alms. His wife of the previous birth was born to the temple priest and named Gouri. Dubaki was born as a male child to the temple owner and named Chenna Basappa. Veerabhadrappa hankered for money in this birth also.

All of a sudden, the cost of the lands went up. The land of Dubaki which the priest presented to his daughter Gouri was sold for rupees one lakh. The value of her jewels also increased hundredfold. As long as their cost was negligible, nobody bothered about them. But when the values shot up, they started quarrelling among themselves. They came to me for advice. I told them that all the property belonged to Lord Mahadev. Therefore it should go to the priest. Since the priest had no sons, all rights accrued to Gouri and no amount should be spent without her permission and her husband had no right to this property. Veerabhadrappa got angry over this and accused me of trying to appropriate the property through Gouri. Hearing his accusation, I prayed to God and kept silent. Veerabhadrappa and Chenna Basappa became enemies over money matters. Veerabhadrappa became wild and threatened Chenna Basappa that he would cut him into pieces. Chenna Basappa sought my protection. I assured him that I would save him from his enemy. After sometime Veerabhadrappa died and took rebirth as a snake. Because of their enmity in their previous birth, the snake tried to eat the frog. To enable me to fulfil my promise, God sent me here and the frog is saved.

Just as in the case of the story of the two goats, we have to learn some important matters from the above story also.

If enmity and unfriendly attitudes were to be our life's aims, then we are bound to come down from the human level to the animal level in our next birth. Therefore, at least for our sake, we should discard these qualities and spend our lives in the path shown by Sai Baba. This is *Prema Marga.*

If anyone misapproriates God's money and uses it for himself or for his family, he will suffer due to acute poverty and will have to beg for his living as in the case of Veerabhadrappa. If the readers hold the posts of Trustees, Secretaries and Treasurers in charge of God's wealth, they should be careful and should not use even a rupee for their personal benefit. In case some have previously used God's money unintentionally, they should reimburse the amount into God's treasury. It is hoped that the readers will take this advice in its correct perspective and become pure in mind and action.

Mrs. Deo's 'Udyapan' Ceremony

Deo was the *tahsildar* of Dahanu in Thane district. He was a Sai devotee as were the members of his family. His mother started a ceremony. She would do *puja* daily for a month and on the last day *Udyapan* ceremony would be held. On that day, according to one's capacity, a number of relatives, friends and devotees would be fed. Deo wanted to celebrate the concluding ceremony on a grand scale by feeding four to five hundred people. While they were discussing the arrangements, his wife suggested that if Shirdi Baba graced the occasion, the reward for the *Udyapan* ceremony would increase a hundredfold and wanted Sai to be invited. Deo immediately wrote to Bapu Saheb Jog who was at Shirdi, to invite Baba on his behalf for the *Udyapan* ceremony. Sitting in Dwarakamai Baba received Deo's invitation through Jog, and said, "I will come running to my devotees who call me with devotion. I will never forget those who remember me always. Whenever anyone thinks of me with love, I will be by their side. I and two others will attend the ceremony.

You write to Deo." After receiving the above message from Jog, all the family members of Deo were very happy. There was still a month's time for the *Udyapan* ceremony.

A *sanyasi* came to the Station Master of Dahan railway station and consulted him on matters regarding collection of donations for the protection of cows. He was dressed like a Bengali gentleman. The Station Master told the *sanyasi* to consult Deo, the *tahsildar*, as he could help him in this matter. Just then Deo also went there and learnt about the *sanyasi's* mission. He told the *sanyasi* that donations were being collected for some other good cause and it was better to come after a month. So he went away.

One month was over. It was the day of *Udyapan* ceremony. The house was full of relatives and friends. In the morning the Bengali *sanyasi* alighted from the *tonga* before Deo's house. Deo recognised and invited him into the house. But the *sanyasi* told him that he had come for meals and not for donations. Deo assured him it was all right and since they are having *Udyapan* ceremony, meals would be served by noon. If the *sanyasi* could tell where he would be, then Deo said he would send someone to fetch him. The *sanyasi* told him that it was not necessary to send anyone. Moreover, Deo would be busy with the work relating to the ceremony. The *sanyasi* finally told Deo that he would come for meals along with two others, and went away.

It was noon. The *sanyasi* came with two youngsters when the meals were in progress and had their meals and went away. The *Udyapan* ceremony went off well. But Deo was not fully satisfied as Baba did not attend the function, in spite of his message that he would attend. He wrote about this to Jog who was at Shirdi. Jog took the letter to Baba. Without seeing or hearing the contents of the letter Baba told Jog that "Sai will never deceive anyone. Having invited me, Deo failed to recognise me, in spite of my telling him that the Bengali *sanyasi* has not come for donations but for meals, there were two more with me and that he need not send anyone to fetch us; we went to his house for meals at the correct time and after taking meals came back." Baba asked Jog to write to Deo about this and to recollect at least now. Then he added, "By doing my *nama smaran,* if you do any good things, there will not be any obstacles. I will always be there for my devotees. It is my duty to look after their welfare. I would rather end my life than break my word."

Baba's 'Padukas' under the Neem Tree in Gurusthan

Dr. Rama Rao Kotari was resident of Bombay. He came to Shirdi in 1912, got attracted to Baba and was in Shirdi for a number of days. He made friends with Dixit, Chandorkar, Shama and others who were with Baba. While discussing matters, they thought that it would be befitting if Baba's *padukas* got carved in stone and put under the neem tree in commemoration of his first visit to Shirdi when he sat under the neem tree. Dr. Kotari sent *padukas* carved out of stone from Bombay. During that period Upasini Baba was staying at Khandoba temple. As per his advise, the *padukas* were brought in a procession on the full-moon day in the month of *Shravana.* That morning at 11 o'clock Dixit brought the *padukas,* carrying them on his head.

From Khandoba temple the procession with musical instruments playing came up to Dwarakamai and after taking the blessings of Baba they were brought to the neem tree and installed under it. The Sai Mahima Shloka *Sada Nimba Vrukshasya Muladhi Vaasaath* written by Upasini Baba was also carved there. From that day onwards puja was being regularly done in Gurusthan. If devotees clean the place and burn incense and *dhoop* on Thursdays, they will get the blessings of God. This was personally told by Baba.

Ratanji Wadia

A Parsee businessman named Ratanji Shapurji Wadia was a resident of Nanded. He had no children. On the advise of Das Ganu, he went to Shirdi and had *darshan* of Sai Baba. He thought of giving five rupees as *dakshina* to Baba. This 'thought' of Ratanji was known to Baba and he asked him to give him five rupees. But immediately, he told Ratanji that he had already received Rs. 3 and annas 14 out of five rupees and therefore he may now give the balance Re. 1 2 annas (16 annas equal one rupee). Ratanji could not recollect when he had given Rs. 3 and annas 14 to Baba. Anyhow, he gave the balance now to Baba as *dakshina.* After thinking for some moments, he understood Baba's statement. When Ratanji wanted to visit Shirdi, a muslim *fakir* named Moula Saheb had come to his house at Nanded. That day Ratanji had spent exactly Rs. 3 and annas 14 in welcoming the *fakir.* As soon as he remembered this, Ratanji thought how great Baba was and there is nothing he did not know. He immediately went and sat near Baba's feet and begged him to give him a child. He developed undeterred devotion to Baba. After sometime he was blessed with a male child.

Baba's Dakshina

Baba took *dakshina* only from a few devotees out of several who came for his *darshan.* Sometimes he accepted when devotees gave him unasked for. But he declined to take from such devotees at other times. He took *dakshina* from all, whether they were rich or poor. He used to ask *dakshina* from women and also children. If any devotee whom Baba had asked for *dakshina* had no money, Baba advised him to take a loan, and give. If a devotee declined to give *dakshina* Baba never got angry. If anyone gave him more than what he asked for, he returned the excess amount. Sometimes he used to give back a portion of the *dakshina* to the devotee with an advice to keep it in the *puja* and worship. At times he took *dakshina* four or five times in a day from the same devotee. There were instances when the devotees gave away the entire amount they had with them. The devotees from whom Baba asked *dakshina* in return received the blessings of Baba. Such devotees never suffered for want of money in their lives. They always thought that Baba asked them *dakshina* for their own good.

Out of the money received through *dakshina,* Baba spent only a little of it for his *chillum* and towards firewood for the Dhuni; the balance amount he gave away to the poor and to those who were with him. Daily he gave away thus up to sixty rupees. The then British Government had received reports through its intelligence agencies, that Baba sometimes distributed more than what he received.

For spiritual progress, generally there are two obstacles: wealth and sex. Baba used to put the devotees to test regarding these two. He asked for money by way of *dakshina.* After that he sent them to the house of Radhakrishna Mai, who was a young and beautiful widow. She used to make arrangements in her house for food for those devotees who came from far-off places. She completely devoted her energies in the services of Baba. Pleased with her devotion, Baba gave her some powers without her knowledge. She could read the thoughts of those who visited her. She used to caution those whose thoughts became perverted after seeing her beauty. Baba sent the devotees to her house at one time or other, just to test them. The devotees exercised utmost caution while in her house.

All the valuable articles that were with Shirdi Samsthan were those brought by devotees on the advise of Radhakrishna Mai. But Baba never showed any interest in them. He told that all that his property consisted of were an undercloth, a separate cloth and a tumbler. His mind never went after materialistic objects. In the same way those who read this *Life History* should develop a detachment from worldy things. With a prayer to Sai Baba to bless these readers with peace and happiness, we will end this chapter.

Om Shanti ! Shanti ! Shantihi !

CHAPTER 22

Baba taught certain things to the devotees who came to him in several ways. There was no separate time or place for that. One day a devotee was abusing another devotee in his absence before others. After sometime, when Baba was going to Lendi Bagh, he met Baba and asked for several things. Baba showed him a pig which was nearby and said, "See how this pig is eating the filth, feeling it tasty. Your behaviour was also like that. You abused a brother devotee with contempt. We got this 'Human Birth' because of the good done in the previous birth. If you do not mend your behaviour, how can Shirdi be of help to you ?" The moral we learn from this is that one should not get elated because of the Sai *puja* done or make several visits to Shirdi. We should not cause any difficulties or harm others under any circumstances. If we indulge in such things, even Baba will not save us.

Sugarless Tea—Cholkar's Story

The famous Kaupeeneswara temple is in Thane district. One day Das Ganu was rendering Baba's *Hari Katha* there and he put Baba's photo on the stage as was customarily done. Hearing the *leelas* and miracles of Baba, Cholkar was pleased and engrossed in it. He was a poor man unable to properly maintain his family. He took a vow that he would visit Shirdi and worship Baba's feet, if he got a steady job. After sometime, he got through a Government examination and was appointed as a clerk in the civil court. As his family was very large, he could not go to Shirdi and fulfil his vow. But he was determined to visit Shirdi and so started saving money. He stopped having sugar in his tea thus saving some amount. After some time he went to Shirdi and had *darshan* of Baba. He fell at the feet of Baba and worshipped him; then out of joy, he distributed sugar candy as Baba's *prasad* to all the devotees.

Cholkar stayed in the house of Bapu Saheb Jog. After noon *arathi* both of them got up to go home. Baba called Jog and told him to put lot of sugar in the tea to be given to his guest Cholkar. Jog could not understand why Baba said this, but Cholkar understood and tears came to his eyes. He understood Baba's omniscience and felt very happy that he had come to Shirdi by saving money. Baba said to him, "If you sincerely pray to me with your stretched hands, I will be with you day and night. Though I am at Shirdi in this form, I know what is happening even beyond the seven seas. Wherever you go in this vast world I will be with you. I dwell in the hearts of my devotees. I am in the hearts of all beings. Whoever realises this will be blessed."

The Story of the Two Lizards

One day, while Baba was seated in Dwarakamai, a lizard on the wall made a noise. A devotee, sitting opposite to Baba, asked him why the lizard was making such a noise. Baba replied that the lizard's sister was expected to come from Aurangabad shortly, and so out of joy, it was making the noise. The devotee kept quiet.

Just then a devotee came on horse from Aurangabad to see Baba. He wanted to feed the horse, and taking out the bag which was with him he shook it. A lizard fell from the bag and rapidly climbed the wall. Baba told the devotee who had questioned Baba earlier, to watch the lizards carefully. The lizard from Aurangabad met her sister and kissed her. They played out of joy, going round and round. People sitting before Baba were very much surprised. Where is Aurangabad? Where is Shirdi? If the lizards were sisters, how did they happen to be at such distances. How did Baba know that the lizard was coming from

Aurangabad? Did he know the mind of animals and also their language? Such doubts arose in the devotees and they simply stared at Baba with surprise.

Baba, who read the minds of the devotees said, "Not only about these lizards, but what is happening in every atom in this world, I know. Without my permission the leaves on the tree also will not flutter. God is all powerful. All should follow the rules of this creation. Even I cannot go against them. God is the creator of all Universe, Allah *Malik hai*."

Baba's Assurance to Bayaja Bai

Bayaja Bai whom Baba addressed as Sister, became physically weak due to old age. She was not in a condition even to get up from bed. Baba ordered Tatya to remain at the bedside of his mother and do service to her. Now and then he would send Tatya's close associates like Shama also to be with Tatya. Bayaja Bai was nearing her end. She wanted to see Baba once. Immediately Baba appeared near her head. His appearance at this last moment gave her divine bliss. Some unexplained joy came to her. She felt that her *Atma* was happily going towards heaven. Perhaps, this feeling was due to the complete divine *darshan* Baba gave her. She wanted to say something but words did not come out of her. She took her son Tatya's hand and put it on Baba's hand. Having understood her thoughts, Baba assured her that he would look after Tatya from that moment more than his life. She knew that his words were God's words. After hearing those words from Baba, her *Atma* left her body and merged in the universe.

Stealing of Rags

B.V. Dev had a desire to read *Jnaneshwari*. The translation of the *Bhagavad Gita* into Marathi by Jnanadev is called *Jnaneshwari* in Maharashtra. This is considered as a very sacred book and many people in Maharastra do *Parayana* of this book regularly. But whenever Dev started to do *Parayana* some obstacles came and he had to stop in the middle. The main reason for this was that he could not fully understand the inner meanings. He went to Shirdi determined to sit before Baba and complete the *Parayana.* Baba asked him twenty five rupees as *dakshina.* Dev gave the amount to Baba but did not ask him about the *Parayana* of *Jnaneshwari.* He went to Sathe Wada and asked a devotee named Balakram Mankar about Baba's *leelas.* When he was narrating some to Dev the following day, Baba called Dev and with angry eyes began scolding him.

He said, "Though you are an old man with grey hairs, you have not stopped stealing. I will kill you with an axe!" Dev shivered. He did not understand anything. Baba asked for twenty-five rupees as *dakshina.* Dev brought the amount and gave it to Baba. This time Baba calmed down and told him, "When I am ready to cover you with a *zari* shawl, why do you steal rags ? You read the *Jnaneshwari.* Sit before me and read it." Immediately Dev started reading the *Jnaneshwari* and finished without any obstacles for the first time. When Baba had threatened to kill him with an axe, the wavering of his mind stopped and he could now concentrate and read the book completely. To ask Balakram about the *leelas* of Baba amounted to stealing of rags. Baba personally showed his greatness, stopping the wanderings of his mind, making him read the *Jnaneshwari,* without any obstacles and increasing his concentration—it was like covering him with a *zari* shawl.

The important thing that we learn from what Baba said is, we should not waste our time and money by running after pseudo Gurus for consultations and advices. "I will give my advice or help, the moment it is sought" is one of the promises of Baba. This assurance is true and valid even now. You must directly ask Baba and have the zari shawl but should not attempt to steal the rags by going to pseudo Gurus.

Sadashiv Tarkhad

Sadashiv worked as a manager in a factory in Bombay. After the factory was closed, he did not have any means of livelihood and so he came to Baba. At that time, Tatya Patil and others were going to Ahmadnagar to see a cinema, with the permission of Baba. Baba asked them to take Tarkhad also along with them for the cinema and from there to proceed to Poona. Tarkhad who was unemployed was surprised at being sent to the cinema. But he knew that none should go against Baba's orders. So, he went to the cinema with the others. When he reached Poona, he found that a factory owner who was trying to secure the services of a person as manager, had heard about him and sent a telegram to his Bombay address, and was waiting for his arrival. So, he got the job immediately. Every advice of Baba was based on one's future.

How to Feed Baba

Ramachander Atmaram's wife, referred to in chapter twenty, was staying with a devotee at Shirdi. One day, during lunchtime, a hungry dog came near her and barked. She threw a bread piece from her plate at the dog, and it ate it quickly and went away, wagging its tail. That evening when she went to Dwarakamai and stood with salutation to Baba, he thanked her for feeding him stomachful. He told her, "In future also you do like this. You first feed the hungry ones and then only take you food. This mosque is my mother. Sitting in her lap I will never tell lies. You should be always kind to me like this. You see me in all living things. You will definitely get higher birth". She was surprised at Baba's words and asked him, "I am myself depending on others in this village for my food. Then when did I feed you?" Baba replied "In the afternoon, before you took your meal, you threw a bread at a dog. I am that dog. I am in all living things like cats, dogs, cows and bees. Those who see me in all are lucky. One should discard the feeling of duality that he is different and animals are different." Baba taught her practically the gist of the *Upanishads*—that one should see God in all living things.

Sai Baba's Teachings

Sai Baba frequently advised on how one should behave in one's daily life. "Because of our contacts in the previous birth, we met each other in this birth also. If any person or animal comes to you, do not drive them away unsympathetically. You should welcome them wholeheartedly and give them due respect. You should give water for the thirsty, food for the hungry and clothing for the naked. God will be satisfied and bless you, if you allow others to take rest in your Verandah. If anyone comes to you for money, you need not give if you do not like to, but you should not abuse or use harsh language and cause pain. This world is like a stage. Carefully observe the several thing being enacted on this stage. But be steady even if the world goes upside down. There is no difference between you and me. We both are one. You remove the wall in between us. God is the Head of all of us. Allah *Malik hai!* None else except God can save us. The method of God is extraordinary very valuable and unimaginable. We all met here because of our tie-up in the previous births. We should be above caste, religion and nationality and move in an affectionate way and be happy and peaceful. We should utilise this body given by God, for the good of others. Such people are only blessed ones. The others live just because they take birth."

Baba taught whenever there was time and opportunity. He used to say that he is omnipresent and present in all elements like earth, air, water, fire and light. He allowed some devotees to do his *pada puja,* some others to hear his *leelas;* some others to go the temple of Khandoba and a few others to do *Parayana* of holy books, according to their needs. He gave instructions to some personally and to some in their dreams. Once, when Radhakrishna Mai was suffering from fever, Baba asked for a ladder to be brought. He climbed it to the roof of her house. He gave two rupees to the person who brought the ladder. Even though all these acts of Baba appeared strange, the fever of Radhakrishna Mai subsided.

Grinding of Wheat

It was the year 1910. Hemadpant came to Shirdi. One day after washing his face, Baba sat in Dwarakamai and started grinding wheat. He lived on alms. He had never done the grinding before. So all who were nearby were looking with wonder at this. Four bold women went inside the mosque, and requesting Baba to sit aside, took the grinding stone and started grinding. Though Baba got angry at this he kept quiet, seeing their affection for him. On completion of the grinding work, the ladies divided the flour into four parts and wanted to take it for themselves. Baba, watching them calmly till then got angry and scolded them, "Oh ladies! Are you crazy? Are you thinking that this flour is your property to take it? I never took any wheat from you. Then why are you taking this flour?" He cooled down after a while and said, "It is all right. Take the flour and sprinkle it on the boundaries of this village." The ladies bowed their heads in shame, touched Baba's feet, went quickly and sprinkled the flour on the boundaries of the village.

The villagers told Hemadpant that there was cholera in the village, and only to eradicate it Baba had done all this. Hemadpant did not understand the relationship between cholera and the wheat flour, but the epidemic in the village gradually subsided. Then Hemadpant concluded that what Baba ground that day was not wheat, but the cholera epidemic which he had sent outside the boundaries of the village. After seeing this *leela* of Baba, Hemadpant desired to write the *Life History of Sai Baba,* containing all the *leelas* and miracles of Baba. He sought the permission of Baba to write the book. But Baba asked him to wait for some time. In the year 1917 Hemadpant tried again through Shama. Baba blessed him and gave *udi prasad. The Life History of Sai Baba* which Hemadpant started writing in Marathi language with the blessings of Sai Baba when he was alive, is read all over the world. This was translated into Telugu by Sri Pratti Narayana Rao.

Sai Baba's Stories—Beacon Lights

In olden days there used to be beacon lights in the high seas. Boats sailing on the seas, with the help of these lights, sailed smoothly without hitting rocks and other dangerous things. This world is also like a big ocean consisting of several types of people with different thoughts and actions. Baba's stories, full of his *leelas,* like beacon lights, show us how to live in this world. These stories are sacred and sweet as nectar, entering our bodies and egos. If the ego is removed, the result is *Jnana.* Through *Jnana* our sins are erased and we attain *moksha.*

Baba's Mercy

On Diwali day in the year 1910, Baba was sitting opposite the 'Dhuni'. He was adding firewood in the Dhuni every now and then. Suddenly, he thrust his hand into the burning Dhuni. The hand burnt. Shama and others who saw this, came running and pushed back Baba, who lost consciousness by then. He appeared to be somewhere else. After sometime, he came to his original state and told the devotees, "A blacksmith's wife living very far off is my devotee. She was working the bellows. When her husband called her, forgetting the child in her lap she got up to run to her husband. The child fell into the burning furnace. I immediately thrust my hand into the furnace and saved it. I am not feeling for my burnt hand. But I am happy that the child of my devotee is saved." How Baba could save a child so far away by putting his hand in the Dhuni at Shirdi is beyond our imagination. That is why we call these actions of Sai Baba as miracles. Sai Baba is a very competent Guru who is capable of doing any work in any manner. I prostrate before Sai Baba for having given me his blessings to write the *Life History* of such a *Samartha Sadguru.* Those who read these stories of Sai Baba are also blessed. Those whose sins are forgiven can only show interest in Baba's stories. This is the Truth.

Bhagoji Shinde's Service to Baba

On knowing that Baba had burnt his hand, Nana Chandorkar brought a notable doctor from Bombay. But Baba declined to get treated by him. He told, God is his doctor. Bhagoji Shinde applied ghee on the burnt hand, and putting some leaves on it bandaged it. This was done by him daily. Though he was a leper he was a very lucky person to have served Baba so closely. For nearly 8 years, from 1910 to 1918, till Baba's Samadhi, he dressed Baba's burnt hand daily.

Damu Anna

A friend of Damodar Savalram Rasne alias Damu Anna from Bombay had written a letter to Damu Anna, that they both jointly do business in cotton as there would be huge profits. Since Damu Anna was a Sai devotee, he wrote to Shama at Shirdi, to take the opinion of Baba on the matter. When Shama went to Dwarakamai to consult Baba about it, Baba told him "What things he is planning! Without being contented with what God has given him, he is trying to earn lakhs of rupees. He is crazy. Let him live happily with half-bread." Shama wrote back to Damu Anna about what Baba had told him. Damu Anna came to Shirdi personally to talk to Baba. He thought of offering him a share in the profits. Baba read his mind and told him that he did not like to involve himself in worldly matters. So Damu Anna dropped the proposal to trade in cotton. Soon after, all the cotton merchants incurred losses. At another time, Damu Anna wanted to trade in paddy. Baba told him that if Damu Anna purchased at 7 seers a rupee he would sell at 9 seers a rupee. As Baba predicted, the rates of paddy came down and all those who hoarded paddy were put to heavy loss. Baba thus saved him twice from heavy losses. Because of this, Damu Anna's devotion to Baba increased and he served him till Baba's *Samadhi*.

He had no children in spite of having two wives. Many astrologers told him that he would not have children. In

1915 someone sent a basketful of mangoes to Baba. He took out four good mangoes from the basket and kept them aside. The rest he distributed to all. But all eyes were on the four mangoes. Having read their thoughts, Baba told them that the four mangoes were for Damu Anna. Just then Damu Anna came to Shirdi. Baba gave him the mangoes and asked him to give them to his younger wife. "You should not eat. She will bring forth four sons and four daughters." After sometime, Baba's words came true and the prediction of the astrologers failed.

The inner meaning of Baba's statement that Damu Anna should eat them and die was that Damu Anna, who felt sad at not having children, would suffer a lot being unable to maintain his eight children at a future time.

Once when Damu Anna was sitting near Baba's feet, he got two doubts. 'So many devotees are coming to Baba. Will all of them be benefited?'

'Now I am seeking Baba's advise in all matters and by acting according to his advice, I am much benefited. But what will be my fate after Baba leaves this body? Should I be like a drifting kite?'

Having read the doubts in Damu Anna, Baba answered, "Look at that mango tree and its thick flowers. If all the flowers become mangoes, how nice it will be. But at the flowering stage itself a lot will fall off. Some will fall off at the stage of tender mangoes. Due to plucking by birds, and children hitting with stones, some more will fall off. Finally very few become ripe mangoes. The same with these devotees also.

"Even after leaving the present body I will be alert. The protection for my devotees will come from my *Samadhi*. I will discharge all my obligations from my *Samadhi*. My bones will look after your welfare."

We pray to Baba, to extend the assurances given to Damu Anna, to the readers of this *Life History* also.

Om Shanti ! Shanti ! Shantihi !

CHAPTER 23

Sai Baba did not encourage the practice of black magic, witchcraft, etc. He never allowed those with such powers to come near him, until they shed off such powers.

Kusa Bhav

Kusa Bhav learnt black magic. The moment he desired, sweets came into his hand. After hearing of Baba's greatness, he came to Shirdi. As he was trying to enter Dwarakamai, Baba stopped him and asked him to give up all his magic powers and only then come to him. For some days he was in a fix not knowing what to do. Finally, he removed the bracelet he was wearing and after giving up the powers, served Baba with devotion for a long time.

On an *Ekadashi* day, someone brought some food made with onions. Baba had no blind beliefs in such matters. He asked Kusa Bhav to eat it. Though Kusa Bhav told Baba that it was *Ekadashi* that day and he did not take onions, Baba insisted on his eating it. Finally Kusa Bhav told Baba that he would eat it if Baba ate too. Then Baba ate first, followed by Kusa Bhav. After a while, some devotees came into the mosque and Baba told them that though it was *Ekadashi* day, and Kusa Bhav, an orthodox Brahmin, had eaten onions. Then Kusa Bhav told them that he had eaten only after Baba had eaten the onions. Baba told that he had not eaten onions but some turnips. So saying he vomited, and the vomit contained pieces of sweet potato instead of onions. Kusa Bhav was surprised at this; he picked up the sweet potato pieces from the vomit and ate them. Baba got angry and scolded him as to why he was doing such a disgusting thing. After a moment Baba's anger turned into pity and he said to him, "I am blessing you. Wherever you are and whenever you want, if you think of me you will get *udi* from Dwarakamai in your hands. If you give *udi* to those in need, their difficulties would be over and their desires fulfilled." From that day onwards till his death, Kusa Bhav used to get handful of *udi* by merely repeating Baba's name. What we learn from this story is that Baba had no liking for black magic. He reformed such devotees who approached him and instead of such lowly powers, gave them some divine powers. Therefore, those who are true devotees of Baba, need not worry about such evil forces. They will not dare to come near them.

Hemadpant

Every Sunday was shandy day at Shirdi. People from neighbouring villages came to Shirdi on that day and visited Sai Baba. Hence, on Sundays at afternoon *arathi,* the mosque would be overflowing with devotees. One Sunday, Hemadpant was pressing Baba's feet. Shama laughingly said to him that there were *chana* sticking to his coat and asked him to see it. When Hemadpant shook his shirt sleeves, a lot of *chana* fell on the floor. Some who were present there picked them up. Hemadpant did not know how the *chana* had come to be on his shirt. Everyone was surprised. Then Baba said, "This person has a bad habit of eating alone. Today is Shandy day. He came here eating *chana.* He is not in the habit of sharing with others. These *chana* seeds are proof of it and what is there to be surprised?"

Hemadpant replied, "Baba, I never eat alone. Why are you putting this allegation on me? Till now I have never gone to the Shandy at Shirdi. I never purchased *chana.* Today also I have neither purchased nor eaten them. I always share with others near me." Immediately Baba said, "You will give to these who are near you. What are you doing when none are near you? Are you thinking of me before you eat anything? I am always with you. Then are you offering me before you eat ?" Hemadpant became dumb at the last question put by Baba. It was true that he not in the habit of offering to Baba before he ate anything. He did not think of this till then. When he considered Baba as everything in his life, was it necessary to offer again whenever he ate? When this doubt came to him, Baba read his thought and proceeded to tell him further.

"Before the sense, mind and intellect enjoy their objects, I should first be remembered, and if this is done, it is in a way making an offering to me. The senses, etc., can never remain without their objects. But if these objects are first offered to the Guru, the attachment to them will naturally vanish. In this way all the thoughts regarding Desire, anger, avarice, etc., should first be offered and directed to the Guru and if this pratice is followed, then God will help you in eradicating all the thoughts. Before enjoyment of the objects, if you think that I am close by, the question whether the object is fit to be enjoyed or not will arise. Then the object that is not fit to be enjoyed will be shunned and in this way your vicious habits or vices will disappear and your character will improve. Then love for the Guru will grow, and pure knowledge will sprout. When this knowledge grows, the body consciousness will go and your intellect will be merged in the spirit-consciousness. Then you will get bliss and contentment. Therefore, you should offer all pleasures you enjoy through the senses to me first. Otherwise, there is the danger that you will not be able to control your senses and will become slaves to your desires."

The above teachings of Baba were not only for Hemadpant, but to all of us, and to the entire world, as long as mankind exists. *The Life History of Shirdi Sai Baba* is full of pearl-like stories. Let this *Life History* be in every household and *Parayana* done regularly. Like the *Mahabharata* and

Ramayana, let this *Life History of Baba* be above caste and religious differences and acquire national character.

Mavisi Bai

Anna Chinchinikar alias Damodar Ganshyam Babre was a devotee of Baba. He was a rough and adamant person. He was very straightforward and frank and did not care for anyone. But he was good at heart.

One afternoon, he was sitting by the side of Baba and massaging his left hand. On the right side of Baba, an old widow by named Venkubai Koujalgi alias Mavisi Bai, sat massaging Baba's back. She was also a person with a pure heart. While massaging due to the movements, her face kept coming very near to that of Anna Chinchinikar. Though she moved forward and backward in the process of massaging Baba's back with full devotion, she complained that Anna Chinchinikar was trying to come very near her with the bad intention of kissing her. At this Anna Chinchinikar got up angrily and tried to quarrel with her. The onlookers were enjoying this quarrel. Then Baba asked them not to quarrel and there was nothing wrong in a son kissing his mother. Thus he cooled down their tempers.

On another occasion Mavisi Bai was massaging Baba's abdomen exerting great pressure. People cautioned her to be careful as there was the danger of the intestines getting damaged. On hearing this, Baba suddenly got angry. His eyes became red. He took his *sataka* and with one end fixed on the pillar in the Dwarakamai, he fixed the other end on his stomach and was trying to thrust it into his stomach with full force. The devotees got scared. Nobody had the courage to talk to Baba or touch him. After sometime Baba came back to his original state. From this story it is clear that Baba knew about the devotion of those who came to him. The devotees served Baba in their own way and there was no need for others to interfere.

Harishchandra Pitale's Son

Pitale was a resident of Bombay. His son was suffering from fits. He was given all types of medicines without any relief. After hearing the *Hari Katha* of Baba rendered by Das Ganu, he came to Shirdi in 1910 with his son. He visited Baba in the mosque and prostrated before him. He put his son near Baba's feet. Baba looked for sometime with concentration at the patient. The boy lost consciousness and fell on the floor. Foam began to come out of his mouth and he perspired profusely, with the temperature of the body going below normal. On seeing the condition of the boy, the parents were very much worried. The boy's mother started weeping. Then Baba told her not to weep but to take the boy to the room and he would be all right in half an hour. After taking the boy to the 'Wada' the boy regained consciousness. From that day onwards the boy did not get fits. While leaving Shirdi, Pitale went to see Baba who told him "Brother, I had given you two rupees on a previous occasion and now I am giving you three rupees. Keep them in your *puja* room and worship them." Since Pitale had come to Shirdi for the first time, he could not understand how Baba could have given him two rupees earlier. After he reached home, when he narrated this to his old mother, She told him, that in the same manner as he had taken his son to Shirdi, his (Pitale's) father had taken him to Akalkot Maharaj. He had given him two rupees and asked him to keep them in the *puja* room and worship them. His father had worshipped them till his death and the worship had stopped after that. From this story it is clear that Sai Baba was Akalkot Maharaj.

Ambadekar

Gopal Narayana Ambadekar, a resident of Poona, suffered without a job for seven years. He came to Shirdi several times and prayed to Baba. Gradually his condition deteriorated. He came then with his wife and stayed for two months.

One night he was sitting in front of Dixit Wada. Unable to bear the financial difficulties, he wanted to end his life by jumping into the nearby well. Just then, the proprietor of the hotel opposite to the Wada, Sagunamer Naik, called him and asked him to read the *Life History of Akalkot Maharaj,* and gave him the book. Ambadekar half-heartedly took the book and opened some page. That page contained the following details.

When Akalkot Maharaj was alive, a person suffered from prolonged illness and unable to bear it jumped into a well to end his life. But Akalkot Maharaj immediately caught hold of him and brought him out of the well, telling him that one had to udergo these difficulties which were a fallout of his actions in the previous birth. Even if one ended his life without fully undergoing the difficulties, in his next birth again he would have to face the difficulties. So before death it was better to suffer for sometime and wipe off the sins of the previous birth. Though he had turned a page of the book at random, the story of an incident similar to his came and Ambadekar took it as an order of Baba and refrained from putting an end to his life.

Gentlemen from Goa

Two gentlemen came to Shirdi from Goa. Baba asked one of them rupees fifteen as *dakshina.* The other person tried to give thirty-five rupees but Baba declined to take them. Shama, who was present there, asked Baba about this discrimination. Baba replied that he himself would never ask for *dakshina.* but Mother Mosque would ask for payment of debt. From whom she desired to have *dakshina,* only from those he would ask. Those who were in debt to her would pay the amount and get salvation. Baba further told that he had no family or property and that he should not accumulate wealth. He took *dakshina* only from those who made certain vows but fell in debt without discharging the vows. One had to undergo the consequences of debt, enmity and killing of others. There was no way of escaping.

The person from one whom now Baba had taken *dakshina* of fifteen rupees was very poor. He took a vow to give the first month's salary to God if he secured a job. He got a job with a salary starting at fifteen rupees. His salary gradually went up to Rs.700. Even then he did not discharge his vow. As a result of his action he was dragged here and Baba had taken the debt money from him.

After this, Baba narrated a story in his usual strange manner. "One day when I was in deep sleep, a person put a hole in the wall and stole Rs.30,000. I was greatly distressed and it upset my mind. I could not drink or eat. Seeing my plight a *fakir* told me, 'I will give you the address of a *fakir*. If you meet him, you will get back your lost money with his help. Till then you should stop taking one of your favourite food items.' I acted according to the advise of the *fakir* and got back my money.

"When I went to board a steamer, there was no room in it. But with the help of a servant working in the steamer I got inside and reached the other shore. From there I travelled in a train and came here." After finishing this story Baba called Shama and asked him to take the two guests for meals. While eating the two gentlemen wept. When Shama asked them the reason, they told him that the story Baba told was their story. The first gentleman said that he had taken a vow to give the first month's salary to Dattatreya. But during the course of time he had forgotten to discharge his vow and Baba reminded him of it, took the amount as *dakshina* and relieved him of the debt. The second gentleman narrated his story as follows. "My cook served me sincerely for 25 years. One day he stole Rs.30,000 from my house. Iwas distressed and weeping. A *fakir* came to our house and told me that if I worshipped Shirdi Sai Baba, I would get my money back. But till then I should not eat my favourite food item. I followed his advise and the cook who stole the money, changed his heart and gave back the entire amount and asked for pardon. For having Baba's *darshan* when we tried to board a steamer at Goa, the captain told us that there is no room. But a servant in the steamer whom we do not know, helped us in getting accommodation and thus we came here." But they how Baba could know of the things which had happened at a very far off place.

The above story proves that Baba was omniscient. Let us pray to Sai Baba to protect us also in all ways. May the readers have complete faith in Sai Baba.

Om Shanti ! Shanti ! Shantihi !

End of Fourth Day's Parayana

FIFTH DAY'S 'PARAYANA'—MONDAY

CHAPTER 24

Baba never fasted. Neither did he permit his devotees to fast. Mind will not be steady if one fasts. We cannot see God with a hungry stomach. It is, therefore, essential to keep the *Atma* satisfied. We get strength for the eyes to see God, for the mouth to praise God and for the ear to hear things about God, only from the energy that food provides. Hence Baba did not approve of fasting.

Fasting by Gokhale's Wife

Gokhale's wife came to Shirdi with some devotees known to Dada Kelkar. She stayed in his house. She desired to undertrake fasting for three days and be with Baba. But Baba told her, "Mother, there is no need to undertake fasting. Go to Dada Bhat's house, prepare *puranpolis* (sweet stuffed chapatis) and feed his children and you also eat." On that day Dada Bhat's wife was indisposed. Hence, Baba's advise appeared to be timely. Accordingly to his advice she prepared *puranpolis,* served the others and ate some. Fasting is only a method of regulating the digestive system and nothing more. To think that one gets some divine benefit from that is only a misconception. Apart from not getting any benefit, fasting makes a person weak, with the result that one cannot attend to one's normal duties. Those who worship Baba can take food and then worship him.

Shama's Vow—Sapta Shringi

The famous Sapta Shringi temple was in a place called Vani in Nashik district. Kakaji Vaidya was the priest of that temple. He suffered one difficulty after another in his life; and there was no peace of mind.

One day he stood in front of the idol and prayed to the Goddess, "I have been worshipping you with utmost devotion and sincerity all these days. Please give me peace of mind." That night the Goddess appeared in his dream and told him, "Go to Baba, you will have peace of mind." The priest thought Baba meant Lord Shiva of Thriambakeshwar. So went there and stayed for ten days, worshipping with devotion. But he did not get peace of mind and returned to his place. Again he prayed to the Goddess and she told him in his dream that she meant Shirdi Sai Baba when she said Baba. The priest was wondering how to go to Shirdi. As he was pious Baba made arrangements for his visit to Shirdi in some other manner.

When Baba's devotee Shama was a small boy he fell sick. His mother took a vow to take the boy to Sapta Shringi temple and worship at the feet of the Goddess. After sometime the mother suffered with ringworm on her breasts and she took another vow to offer the Goddess two silver breasts if the ringworm subsided. Without fulfilling the above two vows she died. This had happened 32 years earlier. Shama had forgotten about this.

Once an astrologer came to Shirdi and told Shama that the vows taken by his mother remained unfulfilled. After thinking over, Shama recollected the two vows. Immediately he got two silver breasts prepared and placing them at Baba's feet, pleaded with Baba to accept them since Baba was also the Goddess Sapta Shringi. Baba did not accept them but asked Shama to go personally to the Sapta Shringi temple and offer them to the Goddess. Shama went to the house of Kakaji Vaidya, the priest of Sapta Shringi, and told him the details.

Kakaji Vaidya thought it a great honour to receive a close follower of Baba from Shirdi. Shama also was pleased meeting the priest through whom the vows are to be fulfilled. Baba might have sent Shama to Sapta Shringi to bring him and Kakaji together. After fulfilling the vows both of them went together to Shirdi. As soon as Kakaji Vaidya touched Baba's feet, his disturbed mind became placid and he felt happy. Baba did not speak anything. He did not even bless him. Even then, by the mere touch of his feet, Kakaji secured peace of mind. Thus Kakaji Vaidya found the greatness of Baba. He stayed for 12 days at Shirdi, experienced Baba's love and left Shirdi taking Baba's *udi* with him.

Shyam Karna—Baba's Horse

A devotee of Baba, who earned huge profits in his business, presented a nice horse to Baba. Baba named it Shyam Sunder (or Shyama Karna) and entrusted its maintenance to a devotee named Tukaram. Many times Baba told the devotees not to merely consider Shyam Sunder as an animal but to treat it as Baba's child.

One day the horse did not eat grass for reasons unknown. Tukaram tried his best but the horse did not touch the grass. He lost his patience and hit it with a stick. This happened a little away from the mosque. Baba sent for Tukaram and asked him angrily why he hit him (Baba) with such a big stick. Tukaram shivered at Baba's words. Then Baba lifted up his long shirt (kafni) and showed a red weal in the shape of a stick on his body. Those who saw it were surprised and feared. They looked at Tukaram suspiciously, but Tukaram told them that he had not come near Dwarakamai on that day and did not hit Baba. Then Baba said, "Is it not hitting me, if you hit my child Shyam Sunder?" He thus made Tukaram remember what he had done. Immediately the devotees ran to the place where the horse was tied. They found a similar swelling and the mark of the stick on the back of the horse. Everyone was surprised. They considered this as Baba's *leela* to prove to the devotees that he was present in all living things. From that day onwards everyone looked after Shyam Karna with love and respect. Some brought fodder for the horse and some brought zari shawls.

A devotee named Aurangabadkar had no children. With Baba's blessings he got a male child. Out of gratitude constructed a shed for he Shyam Karna at a cost of Rs.500. Every Thursday they decorated Shyam Karna nicely and put it in front of the procession. The horse danced to the tunes of the musical instruments.

Testing Baba

It was the year 1915. One Thursday morning, the mosque was full of devotees. Baba was sitting with crossed legs on the big stone in front of the mosque. Nana Chandorkar, Shama, Mhalsapathi, Dixit, Tatya, Sathe and others were standing. A rich middle-aged lady, Janaki Bai, wearing a silk saree with zari border, brought several costly items of jewellery on a gold plate to give them to Baba. She was standing in the ladies' queue. Every devotee had something or the other in his hand to hand it over to Baba. Some washed the feet of Baba by placing them in a silver plate. Some applied sandalpaste on his neck and sprinkled perfumes. Some offered flowers, fruits and *pedas.* (a milk sweet). Some offered money according to their capacity.

Nanavali, who was standing behind the devotees, observed all this and felt happy. But in a few moment his face changed and his happiness disappeared. His face flushed with anger. His eyes became red and his appearance was fearful. He called out in a very loud voice, "You fakir!" All looked towards him, stunned. Nanavali slowly advanced towards Baba and was stared into his eyes. He was a rough type of person and everyone feared what was to happen. He said to Baba, "So many here have got up and stand fearing me. But you are calmly sitting cross-legged." Baba did not reply. Nanavali ordered Baba to get up. Baba went and stood near the devotees. Nanavali sat cross-legged on the stone just like Baba. He ordered the devotees to bring the offerings to him. He ate some and threw away some. He stared for some time at the lady who had brought jewels in a gold plate. He stared alternately at the lady and the gold plate for some time. Finally he looked at her insultingly and spat.

Then he looked at Baba and said, "What Nawab! How are you?" Baba replied that he was a fakir only and not a nawab. Nanavali questioned Baba about how the world was. Baba replied, "It is as usual." Nanavali asked what Baba meant by his reply. Then Baba said, "With the five elements and eight directions this world appears normal only to me." With this reply Nanavali's face changed, his anger disappeared and he became normal again. Again he stared into Baba's eyes. Their eyes exchanged something silently. Nanavali fell at Baba's feet and asking pardon went away quickly to the relief of the devotees.

Then Nana Chandorkar said to Baba. "Baba, the crazy actions of Nanavali are increasing day by day. He dared to sit on your seat and spoiled the offerings brought by the devotees, and also insulted your devotees. We will not tolerate this further. If you permit us we will take appropriate action." To this Baba replied, "Nanavali is not a crazy person as all of you are thinking. He is a sage *(avadhuta)* who crossed the worldly limits. He had come to test me." Then Nana Chandorkar asked Baba how a crazy person could test him. Baba explained as follows, "When I came to Shirdi for the first time, the villagers threw stones at me taking me to be a crazy person *(pagal fakir)*. After sometime they called me a doctor. Now you are all treating me as God and worshipping me and offering me several things. Nanavali only tested me to find out whether desires have sprouted in me on seeing all this. From the reply I gave him he understood that I am in the original state only and nothing has changed in me. Craziness is the climax of

Vedanta." In the light of Baba's explanation, the devotees recollected the questions and answers between Nanavali and Baba and felt happy. From that day they wiped out their opinion that Nanavali was a crazy person.

Red Plantains

Shri M.G.Rege visited Baba during his student days. In those days, he was the youngest of all devotees who were close to Baba. One day a devotee presented Baba with plantains whose outer skin was red in colour. Rege was attracted by the red-coloured peel of the plantains. He desired to eat them. Baba gave the plantains to the devotees who were there. He removed the outer skin of a plantain and while he gave the inner fruit to a devotee, he gave the outer skin to Rege and asked him to eat it. Obeying Baba's orders, he ate the skin. After distributing to all, Baba came to Rege and took out another plantain, peeled the skin and threw it away. He shared the inner fruit along with Rege. Since Rege had been attracted by the red colour of the plantain skin, Baba had made him eat it and know the taste. He again gave him the inner fruit to bring home the truth that there is nothing in the outer colour but the actual taste is in the inner fruit. So, one should not be carried away by the external appearances but should see the divine power in every matter.

Om Shanti ! Shanti ! Shantihi !

CHAPTER 25

Upasini Shastri went to Nagpur, form there to Scinde and to Khargapur in the year 1914, without informing Baba and without completing the four years novitiate *(diksha)* prescribed by Sai Baba. Afterwards he stayed with Panchamuni for some time. By Baba's grace he acquired *siddhis* (supernatural powers) while he was at Shirdi. After wandering about for 15 months, he returned to Shirdi in the year 1915, and Baba advised him to set up an *ashram* at Sakori, a village near Shirdi and live there. He followed Baba's advice. Those who were sufferers, patients, etc., came to Upasini Baba in thousands and obtained relief. He was Guru to a number of devotees, and attained *Samadhi* in the year 1942 at the age of 72. Those who go to Shirdi can also visit the ashram established by Upasini Baba at Sakori, which is about 5 kms from Shirdi.

Importance of Actions

Baba went for alms everyday. With the increase of Baba's greatness, the faith in those who gave alms also increased and they kept the food ready and waited for Baba.

One day, a housewife named Savitri Bai was hurriedly cooking as the time of Baba's visit for alms was nearing. Her old father-in-law was also hungry as cooking. She finished cooking quickly. As she was putting *rotis* (leavened bread) and curry in a plate to give to Baba, he arrived and she asked him to just wait for two minutes and she would be bringing food for him. In the meantime, her father-in-law called out loudly as he was hungry. She told him that she would serve him as soon as she had given food to Baba. She came out of the house with the food in a plate to give it to Baba. Baba told her, "Mother, you should give food to your father-in-law first. You may ask me why. To give food to your father-in-law is your duty. To give me alms is only a pious action. You should give precedence to duty over noble action! To give timely food to your father-in-law is righteousness *(dharma);* you should attend to that first. After that only alms for me." Hearing Baba, she told him that he was really God in human form and her desire was to serve him first. Baba further told her, "Our actions are very powerful and are like arms *(aayudhas).* God has kept your father-in-law under your care and made you responsible to serve him. Even if such a God stood before your house, you should give priority to your duties only. This is the Theory of Karma. What duties God has given us, we should discharge them properly. If you do not do them properly, it amounts to wrong. It is not proper for me to make you, who reposed complete faith in me, do wrong. In my presence give food to your father-in-law. Till then I will sit and wait here. Afterwards I will accept the food you proposed to give me with love." Thereupon she acted as per Baba's advice. From that day onwards, Savithri Bai always gave food to her father-in-law before Baba came for alms.

Baba's Knowledge of Sanskrit

Sai Baba was a strange God. Shirdi is a *punya bhoomi* for having had such a God there. The villagers of Shirdi are blessed. Even the grass on which Baba walked is also blessed. Shirdi came into prominence because of Baba. All *siddhis* (supernatural powers) were at the feet of Baba. Those who visited Shirdi worshipped Baba's feet. One day, Nana Chandorkar, while pressing Baba's feet, recited within himself some *shloka.* None were there. Baba asked him what he was reciting to himself. Chandorkar replied that it was a Sanskrit *shloka* which Baba would not understand. Baba said that he would try to understand and asked Chandorkar to read it aloud. He read the thirty-fourth shloka in chapter 4 of the *Bhagavad Gita* as follows:

Tatviddhi Pranipatena Pariprashnena
Sevaya - Upadekshyanti Te Jnanam
Jnanina Stattwadarshinah

The questions of Baba and the replies of Nana Chandorkar were as follows:

Baba: Nana, What is the meaning?

Nana: By making *sashtanga namaskar* (prostration), questioning the Guru, serving him, we learn what this *jnana* is. Then these *jnanis* who have attained the real knowledge of Brahman, will give us *upadesha* of *Jnana.*

Baba: I do not want this collective purport of the whole stanza. Give me word by word meaning of it. What is meant by *pariprashna?*

Nana: Asking questions.

Baba: What is the meaning of *prashna?*

Nana: The same (asking questions).

Baba: For both you are giving the same meaning. Is there any special meaning for the Sanskrit word *pari?*

Nana: I do not know of any other meaning.

Baba: What is meant by *seva?*

Nana: The same service that we are doing to you daily.

Baba: Is it enough to render such service ?

Baba: In the shloka, suppose we substitute the word *Jnana* with *Ajnana,* then what meaning does it give?

Nana: I do not understand how to construe it by substituting with *Ajnana.*

Baba: Lord Krishna was a *Tatwadarshi.* But why did he advise Arjuna to prostrate, serve, and question other *Jnanis?*

Nana: This also I do not understand.

Nana Chandorkar thought Baba did not know Sanskrit and that he (Nana), having read the *Bhagavad Gita* several times along with commentaries, knew everything. But when Nana could not give answers to Baba's questions for even one *shloka,* he felt ashamed. Then he concluded that however much one might have read, one cannot be equal to a *Jnani.* His pride had gone. Then Baba in his own style, gave answers to the questions he had put to Nana, as follows:

1) Questioning the Guru should not be for testing the Guru or trying to trap him, but to actually learn and to keep in mind what was learnt, and to put that in practice in life. One should question the Guru with the aim of spiritual progress. That is what is meant by *Pariprashna.* Vyasa did not use it for nothing.
2) *Seva* or service which is rendered whenever you feel like doing, is not *seva.* A person should feel that his body is not his and God had given it to serve the Guru. Persons with such *Jnana* only can understand the teaching of it by a Guru, and others cannot understand. To teach *Jnana* to such persons would be like teaching *Ajnana.*
3) However great a person may be, his close associates cannot gauge his greatness, taking him to be an ordinary human being like them.

This is the effect of *Maya.* That was the reason why Lord Krishna advised Arjuna to serve other *Tatwadarshis.*

After hearing the above explanations given by Baba, Nana could not imagine the greatness of Baba who had such deep knowledge of the *Bhagavad Gita* which Lord Krishna taught to Arjuna. He learnt that the sky was the limit for Baba's knowledge, and none could measure it. He thought how much small he was before Baba. Noticing the changes taking place in Nana, Baba slowly walked out of Dwarakamai. Nana also came out of Dwarakamai, following Baba in the same manner as an iron piece is attracted by a magnet. Nana saw Baba's form growing big with changes in his face, with divine light rays emitting from his body in different colours. He had to lift his head to see the growing stature of Baba. He had to close his eyes, unable to withstand the divine light coming from Baba.

He heard Baba's bold and loud words as if they came from the sky above. "Nana, your eyes contained the human body and caught in the darkness of *Ajnana,* cannot see my divine form. I am giving you divine sight. Open your eyes and see my real form. I am the divine power and the bearer of all the planets. Sun and moon are my eyes. I am the *Virat* and send the people either to heaven or hell based on their actions in life. The burning planets, oceans, all kinds of diseases, medicines required for their cure are all in me. All the animate and inanimate things of this creation are in me. There is nothing which is not in me. I am a complete being and all powerful person."

Hearing Baba's words and seeing his *Vishwarupa,* Nana became unconscious for a moment. When he came back to his original state, he saw Baba in his usual form. Baba cautioned Nana not to reveal to others what he had seen. Nana was in a confused state not knowing whether what he had seen was a dream or real or whether it was *Maya.* When he found himself in control of his senses, he concluded that he was not dreaming. He fell at the feet of Baba and washed them with the tears that fell with joy.

Nanas' Disrespect for the Temple

Once Nana Chandorkar, along with his relative Binivalle, came to Shirdi. Baba asked him, "Being with me for such a long time, why did you do this? How did you come to Shirdi from Kopargaon?" Nana recollected the mistake committed by him. Whenever he came to Shirdi from Kopargaon, he used to bathe in the Godavari river, visited Datta temple and then come to Shirdi. During his previous visit he had promised the temple priest that he would give Rs. 300 as donation. Thinking that the priest would ask him the money if he visited the temple, he avoided it and also discouraged his relative from visiting the temple. Baba, knowing the matter beforehand, said to Nana, "If you had no money to fulfil your promise, you could have told the temple priest. For money's sake you could not visit Datta Dev. See how money has distanced you from God." Realising his mistake, Nana bowed his head in shame.

Arathi and Naivedya (Offerings to God)

Everyday after the noon *arathi,* all devotees went back to their houses or to the lodgings. Baba personally distributed *udi prasad* and made enquiries about each devotee, giving them advices. From some devotees he would enquire when they came and to some devotees he would ask when they would be leaving Shirdi. He ordered a few devotees to leave Shirdi only the next day. He enquired with some devotees about some who were in their houses and gave some advices. He talked to the devotees to the extent necessary and according to their needs. Only he and the particular devotee could understand the matter. After the devotees left, the devotees close to Baba would sit in rows on each side of him. Baba would come walking slowly and sit in his seat.

Those who brought offerings to Baba *(naivedya)* waited outside Dwarakamai, for getting his blessings. They would bring a variety of food items like *rotis,* sweet rice, *sanja,* etc. All the offerings were kept before Baba and he offered all of them to God. After that he distributed a portion of them to the devotees waiting outside the mosque and the balance served to all the close devotees who were sitting on either side of Baba. The food items touched by Baba became very tasty and energy-giving ones.

One day, Hemadpant ate such food to his satisfaction. Baba immediately gave him a glassful of buttermilk and asked him to drink it. But Hemadpant drank only a little of it saying that his stomach was full. Its taste was peculiar. Baba asked him to drink the balance also, as such an opportunity would never come again. He drank the remaining buttermilk with great difficulty. His word became true. Hemadpant did not get such a chance again before Baba's *Samadhi.*

Atmaram's Wife

Atmaram's wife desired to offer three items to Baba as *naivedya:* (1) Brinjal and curd chutney, (2) Brinjal fried curry, and (3) *peda* (a milk sweet).

Raghuveer Purander's wife was known to her. When Mrs. Purander was going to Shirdi, Atmaram's wife gave her some brinjals with a request to prepare the chutney and curry and serve Baba. After reaching Shirdi, Mrs. Purander prepared the brinjal and curd chutney and sent it to Dwarakamai at Baba's meal time. As the preperation was tasty, Baba distributed it to all. He desired to have brinjal fried curry also then and there. As that was not the season for brinjals, Radhakrishnamai made enquiries as to who had brought the brinjal curd chutney and found out that it was Mrs. Purander. Word was sent to her about Baba's desire and immediately Mrs. Purander prepared brinjal fried curry and sent it to Baba. The devotees who came to know the details of the matter were surprised at the desire of Baba to have brinjal fried curry. This is one more instance of Baba's omniscience.

In December 1915, Balaram Mankad, a resident of Bandra, was going to Shirdi to perform the obsequies of his late father. Atmaram's wife wanted to send something to Baba and searched in the house but could not find anything. A few pieces of *peda* were there. Even these few were already offered to Baba as *naivedya.* She sent them with Mankad. After reaching Shirdi, Mankad forgot about them when he went to see Baba in the afternoon. Again when he went to the mosque in the evening, Baba asked Mankad what was given by Atmaram's wife at the time of his journey to Shirdi. Mankad felt ashamed and went to his room and brought the *pedas* given by Atmaram's wife and gave them to Baba. Baba took one and ate it and the remainder were distributed to others.

Importance of Human Birth

For all living things, food, sleep, fear and reproduction are common. But a human being, apart from these, has one more important quality called intelligence *(jnana)*. With this the human is able to know about God. Some think that the human body comprises flesh, blood, and filthy waste products. The body finally dies and gets destroyed. Even then, through this body only we are able to get *Jnana*. Hence, good care should be taken to maintain a healthy body. If one indulges in pleasures and yields to physical desires, life will ultimately become lower than that of an animal. So one should take necessary care. If excess care is taken, this will lead to several desires and if less care is taken, it will result in poor health and will lead to some diseases.

One should understand this truth carefully. Finally the body should be utilised for obtaining *moksha*.

Khushal Chand of Rahata

Baba loved Khushal Chand of Rahata very much. When sometimes he went to Rahata with devotees, Khushal Chand welcomed Baba from the entrance to Rahata with drums, cymbals and other musical instruments and took them in a procession. He arranged food for all others also. After taking food, Baba and Khushal Chand would discuss several matters. Similarly, Baba used to go up to Neemgaon and Kopargaon occasionally. He never went beyond these places. But he did know of the happenings at other far off places.

Khaparde's Wife

While Khaparde and his wife were at Shirdi, his wife used to take food for offering to Baba daily at noon time. She took food only after Baba accepted her offering. Baba was pleased at her steady and deep devotion and faith in him.

One day, she brought food as usual. Baba took the plate and began eating. Then Shama, who was present there, asked Baba why he was showing discrimination among the devotees. "So many devotees bring you offerings of food. You don't touch them. But you are eagerly taking the food brought by Khaparde's wife and eating it quickly. What is the speciality in her offering?"

Baba replied, "The food brought by her is really tasty. In her previous birth she was the cow of a merchant. She gave good milk to the satisfaction of the merchant's family. In her subsequent birth, she was born as daughter to a gardener and served others well. Because of her nobility, in the next birth she was born to a kshatriya (a caste) and married a merchant. In this birth also she is serving others sincerely and because of this, in her next birth, she will be born to a Brahmin family. I have seen her after a long period. Let me take some more food filled with love from the *naivedya* brought by the lady." So saying Baba finished all the food that was in the plate and went and sat on his seat. Khaparde's wife began massaging his feet and he in turn started massaging her hands. The way the Guru and pupil were serving each other caused much surprise and also happiness to the devotees present there. Baba fixed his eyes on her and looked at her seriously; some divine power entered her. She shed tears out of joy. Baba advised her to repeat the mantra 'Raja Ram' always, and that it would bring peace and happiness to her and she would achieve her life's desire.

Those who serve their Guru with a pure mind and love, will earn the love of their Guru. In fact, a Guru will depend on such disciples only. Such teacher-disciples are in fact one only and there will be no differences among them. Let us pray to Sai Baba to turn all those readers who read this *Life History,* into such *sishyas,* and thus close this chapter.

Om Shanti ! Shanti ! Shantihi !

CHAPTER 26

The real name of Radhakrishnamai was Sunderbai Ksheersagar. She came to Shirdi in the year 1907 and completely dedicated herself to Baba's service. Before her arrival at Shirdi, Balaji Sevalkar used to clean the paths on which Baba walked and also the front space before Dwarakamai and Lendi Bagh. Later, Radhakrishnamai attended to this work. She devoted herself with body, mind and soul in Baba's service, for nearly 9 years till her death in 1916. She had no other thoughts except serving Baba. After her death, a Muslim devotee, Abdullah, attended to the work done by Radhakrishnamai. Tatya Kote Patil also served Baba with love. Tatya's duties were to changing Baba's dress, serve Baba with tasty food arrange soft mattresses one over the other for Baba to sleep. If sometimes Baba did not do as told, Tatya somehow coaxed him and if necessary by undertaking fast, made Baba do as he was told. The mutual love between Baba and Tatya appeared like the uncle-nephew relationship.

Baba slept in Chavadi on alternate days. On such days he and Venkusa talked over several matters. The eastern side of Chavadi was set apart for Venkusa, as per his wish and none were permitted to sleep there. Ladies were not allowed to enter this portion but only the western side portion and after visiting Baba, they had to leave immediately. Thursdays were important to Baba's devotees. Baba who gave much importance to the Guru tradition told them that Thursday *(Guruvar)* was very dear to him. Thus, the importance to Thursday started from then onwards. In the beginning Chavadi Utsav was celebrated once in two days. Afterwards, it was celebrated once a week on Thursdays. This Utsav attracted a large number of devotees who participated with joy and danced with full abandon. We shall now go into these details.

Chavadi Utsav

On Utsav night, devotees gathered near the front side of the mosque and sang *bhajans* (singing of devotional songs accompanied by musical instruments) for sometime. Behind the bhajan party was the chariot, on their right side was the tulsi plant and to their front was Baba. The lighted torches for the procession were got ready. Some said loudly now and then with devotion "Sainath Maharaj Ki Jai". Lights were lit all around the mosque and buntings tied. While these arrangements went on, Tatya would come to Baba and ask him to get ready. Baba's horse Shyam Karna, gaily decorated, would be kept ready for the procession.

Baba, putting on his upper cloth, carrying the *sataka* under the arm and also the *chillum* along with tobacco, would get ready to go. Tatya brought a *zari* shawl and it put around Baba's shoulders and lifted him up slowly. After getting up, Baba would go near the Dhuni, push the firewood with the toe of his right foot and with his right hand put, out the lamp in the mosque, turning in all directions, appearing to talk to someone by making gestures. Perhaps, he was talking to his mother Dwarakamai! After this he would come down the steps of Dwarakamai and the devotees would cry out "Shri Sainath Mahraj Ki Jai". Some devotees on either side of Baba would wave the *chamaras.* Lengths of white cloth were spread throughout on the path on which Baba walked. Tatya would hold Baba's left hand, while Mhalsapathi his right hand. Bapu Saheb Jog would hold a *zari* silk umbrella over Baba's head. Baba's horse Shyam Karna' would be in the front of the procession. The bhajan party were behind the horse, with different kinds of musical instruments.

After proceeding for about 10 or 15 feet, Baba's sight would wander somewhere else. He appeared to be talking to somebody and making gestures. Perhaps Gurudhan, Dwarakamai and Venkusa were also there in the procession along with Baba! Baba also appeared to be talking and making gestures to Hanuman in the Maruthi Mandir to the left. When the procession reached halfway, the facial expressions of Baba changed. He appeared shining and emitting bright light like the morning sun. Sometimes he used to look with piercing eyes at some of the devotees, and their fears, sufferings and diseases would disappear. The devotees would become joyous and Mhalsapathi would dance as if in a trance. Tatya used to shed tears of joy at this sight. But Baba appeared unmoved by all this and was steady. Dixit used to shower flowers and *gulal* on Baba.

In this manner, as soon as the procession reached the main entrance to Chavadi, Bapu Saheb Jog washed the feet of Baba in a silver plate, applied sandalpaste and gave *arathi* with camphor. Then Baba was slowly taken inside and made to sit on a bed made up with several mattresses. Then Shama prepared *chillum* and gave it to Tatya. After smoking once, Tatya gave it to Baba. It was then given to Mhalsapathi after Baba smoked. This act showed oneness. In this way the Utsav ended and some devotees put garlands on Baba. Baba had no desire for all these. But he agreed to all these for the satisfaction of the devotees. Finally, Bapu Saheb Jog gave full *arathi* and the devotees went back to their places. After making all arrangements for Baba, Tatya took leave of Baba, and while permitting him to go Baba asked him to come once during the night and see him. Tatya did as asked. After all the devotees left, Baba used to make a bed with 50 or 60 bed sheets, one over the other and slept. That was Yoga Sleep. But, for Baba it was not real sleep. If Baba slept then the entire world will slept.

Sai devotees, while going to bed, are advised to recollect the Chavadi Utsav and imagine themselves to be in the procession. Then they will be nearer to Baba and it would be possible to see him in their dreams.

Om Shanti ! Shanti ! Shantihi !

CHAPTER 27

Accepting *dakshina* by Baba commenced in the year 1907, with few pice (coppers). In the years 1912-1916, Baba used to get Rs. 500 per day as *dakshina.* But Baba used to distribute this amount by evening to the needy and those who were dependent on him. Sathe established a society, "Dakshina Biksha Sanstha", in 1915, for the propagation of Sai *leelas* and miracles. This Sanstha gathered several matters relating to Baba and published them.

Baba's Pilgrimage to Gaya

Kaka Saheb decided to perform the thread ceremony of his son at Nagpur. At the same time Nana Chandorkar's eldest son's marriage was fixed to be celebrated at Gwalior. Both came to Shirdi and invited Baba to attend the functions. Baba asked them to take Shama as his representative. But they insisted that Baba should come personally. He asked them to take Shama along with them and he would reach Gaya, before Shama finished his pilgrimage of Kashi and Prayag and reached Gaya.

Shama went to Nagpur as Baba's representative for the thread ceremony of Kaka Saheb's son. From there he went to Gwalior for the marriage of Nana Chandorkar's eldest son. Afterwards he went on pilgrimage to Kashi and Ayodhya and from there reached Gaya in the third month. Having come to know that there was plague in Gaya, he feared. He stayed with a *panda* at Gaya. On seeing a big photo of Sai Baba in the *panda's* house, he was surprised. He remembered Baba's words that he would reach Gaya even before he reached the place and he shed tears out of joy on seeing Baba's photo there. The *panda* told him that when he had gone to Shirdi for Baba's *darshan* 12 years back a Sai devotee named Shama had given him the photo of Sai Baba. Shama recollected this and told the *panda* that he was the same Shama who had given him the photo. The *panda* was very much pleased to have him as his guest.

Sapatnekar and His Wife

Sapatnekar was a resident of Akalkot. When he was studying law, a co-student of his by name Shevade used to get low marks. Shevade told him that though he got low marks then, now he would get good marks and pass in the final examination with the blessings of Shri Shirdi Sai Baba. On hearing this, Sapatnekar made fun of Shevade as well as Sai Baba.

After 15 years, Sapatnekar's only son died. He became disheartened and visited several holy places but could not get peace of mind. He finally came to Shirdi for Baba's *darshan.* Baba did not allow him inside the mosque. He tried twice or thrice but every time Baba asked him to get out. He became helpless and went back home.

After some time, Baba appeared in the dream of Sapatnekar's wife. In the dream Sapatnekar's wife was going with a pot on her head to fetch water. A fakir met her on the way and told her that he would fill the pot with water. Considering this as a good omen, Sapatnekar and his wife went to Shirdi immediately.

After seeing Baba she told her husband that was the same *fakir* who had appeared in her dream. Because of her good behaviour and devotion, Baba called her and told her following in his usual style: "My stomach, waist, hands and legs are paining since several days. In spite of using several medicines, there is no relief. After coming here the pains have subsided." Even though Baba did not reveal the name, the story was about her she realised. Thinking this was the appropriate time, Sapatnekar worshipped Baba's feet with folded hands. This time also Baba asked him to go out. Sapatnekar realised that this was the result of his insulting his friend Shevade and Baba. With repentance in him, he again fell at Baba's feet. This time Baba blessed him with his hand put on his head and stroked it.

While Sapatnekar was pressing Baba's feet, Baba narrated a story about a person and his sufferings—it was Sapatnekar's story. Baba told the devotees who were by his side: "This man is blaming me for his son's death. Will I kill other's children? He is sitting on the lap of this mosque mother and weeping. I will put the boy who died, again in his wife's womb." Then he told Sapatnekar, "These feet of mine are very holy. They are also old. Your difficulties are over. You be calm and without any worry." Next day Baba took two rupees as *dakshina* from Sapatnekar. He gave a coconut to him and asked him to put it in the lap of his wife. He told him to be fearless and go back home. After a year they were blessed with a son.

Somadeva Swamy

Somadeva Swamy from Haridwar was coming to Shirdi in the year 1912. From a distance he saw the flags on the mosque. A *yogi* (saint) who shows interest in the flags is interested only in name and fame and there is no need to visit such a *yogi,* so thought Somadeva Swamy and wanted to turn back without seeing Baba. But his co-passengers in the tonga persuaded him to visit Baba, having come all the way. They also told him that actually Baba was not interested in the exhibition of flags etc. Somadeva Swamy changed his mind and went for a *darshan* of Baba. As soon as he had *darshan* from a distance, all his prejudices vanished, his heart melt and eyes filled with tears of joy. His throat dried up. He was eager to dedicate his life to the service of Sai Baba. When Somadeva Swamy went into the mosque and tried to touch Baba's feet, Baba said to him, "Let our pomp and show be with us. You go home. Do not come to the mosque. Why should you have the *darshan* of a *yogi* who is fond of flying flags on the mosque? Don't stay even for a minute." Somadeva Swamy understood that Baba was reflecting the thoughts he had at the beginning. He took the words of Baba as his blessings. Afterwards he became a great Sai devotee.

Message for the Construction of Samadhi Mandir

Sreeman Baba Saheb Butty, a millionaire from Nagpur, was living in Shirdi along waith his family in August, 1913. He wanted to build a 'Wada' like Sathe and Dixit Wadas. Baba never talked about things he intended to do. But when the time and opportunity came he used to get things done tactfully.

One night when Butty and Shama were sleeping in Dixit Wada, Baba told them in their dream, to build a Wada for Sri Krishna temple. Shama, unable to control his joy, wept. Butty, being a wealthy and competent person and above all this a faithfull devotee of Baba, commenced the arrangements for building the temple. A plan was prepared by Shama with a big hall in the centre and rooms on all sides, with Lord Krishna's idol to be placed in the hall. This model plan was shown to Baba and his approval obtained. Arrangements were made for the commencement of the temple construction, starting with the foundation ceremony.

Tendulkar's Family

The Tendulkars lived in Bandra and all the members of the family were Sai devotees. Tendulkar's son was studying hard to appear for medicine. But he was unable to concentrate on his studies and was fearing that he might not be able to get through in the examinations. The astrologers who examined his horoscope expressed their opinion that the planets were in adverse position in that year and it would be very difficult to pass the examinations. In such circumstances, Savithri Bai, wife of Tendulkar went to Shirdi for Baba's *darshan.* She raised her son's topic with Baba. He told her, "Ask him to keep faith in me and study carefully and not to get disheartened. Let him put aside the horoscopes and palmistry and keeping faith in me write the examinations. He will definitely pass the examinations." Tendulkar's son kept complete faith in mother-like Baba and got through in the examinations. Baba's words proved correct while astrology failed. From this we learn that Baba's words are above all *shastras.* Any word coming from his mouth will happen without fail. There is no question of Baba's words failing.

The above-mentioned boy's father was Raghunath Rao Tendulkar. He was working in Bombay for a foreign company. Due to old age he could not discharge his duties properly and thought of resigning. He was getting a salary of Rs.150 p.m. So, he would get a pension of Rs.75 p.m. He was fearing that with his meagre pension he would not be able to maintain his family. Baba appeared in Savitri Bai's dream, asked whether a pension of Rs.100 would be sufficient. The management of the company decided to give him a pension of Rs.110 p.m. This happened because of Sai's grace only.

Captain Hatey

Captain Hatey was a resident of Bikaner and a Sai devotee. One day Baba appeared in his dream and asked him whether he had forgotten him. Captain Hatey asked how a mother could forget her child, and how she could live forgetting the child. So saying he brought a bottlegourd from the garden, prepared curry with it and offered to Baba. Suddenly he woke up. After a few days, he gave Rs.12 to a friend who was going to Shirdi and requested him to get the curry prepared with the bottlegourd for Rs.2 and give Rs.10 to Baba as *dakshina.* His friend did as requested by Hatey. When he took the curry to Baba, he ate only the curry and forsook his meals that day. Knowing this, Captain Hatey, felt extremely happy.

On another occasion, Captain Hatey, desirous of worshipping the coin touched by Baba, sent one rupee through his friend to Shirdi. The friend gave the rupee coin to Baba without mentioning anything. Baba examined the coin turning it this side and that side. With the thumb of the right hand he played for some time by sending the coin up. Afterwards he gave back the coin to Hatey's friend with instructions to gives it back to the owner along with *udi,* and also to inform him that Baba did not require anything from him. He further told him to inform the owner to keep cool and be happy. Captain Hatey started worshipping the coin daily.

Baba used to say to devotees that if their heart was like a mirror, he was the image in the mirror. He said several times that he depended on sincere and pious devotees only. What he required was the devotees' love and affection and not wealth. Therefore the devotees should sincerely repose their faith in Baba and not spend huge amounts of money in fulfilling their vows. They should offer their mind, intellect and thoughts to Baba and dedicate their life to him.

Om Shanti ! Shanti ! Shantihi !

End of Fifth Day's Parayana

SIXTH DAY'S 'PARAYAN'—TUESDAY

CHAPTER 28

Butty Wada

Sreeman Butty, with the help of Shama, Kaka Saheb Dixit and others, had procured the material required for the construction of the Wada, and engaged the required workers. They decided to commence the work on 30 December 1913 with the laying of the foundation stone. Baba also agreed to this. The construction started. Shama was supervising. The underground structure, the outside structure and digging of the well were completed. Baba also saw the construction work daily on his way to Lendi Bagh and back to the mosque. Sometimes Baba would indicate some alterations and give some suggestions. Slowly the workers also developed devotion and faith in Baba. They saluted Baba every day before the commencement of work and also at closing time. The building material and the implements were taken care of by Bapu Saheb Jog. With Baba's blessings, the building rose quickly. The workers worked as if it was a holy *yagna.*

Butty was in a hurry to install Sri Krishna's idol in the big hall. When he sought permission of Baba to order for the idol, Baba declined to give the permission, stating that when the Wada was completed, he would himself come and reside there and all of them would embrace each other and play there and be happy. On another occasion, Baba sat cross-legged on the 'base' constructed for installing Sri

Krishna's idol. Butty once again asked Baba's permission to get the idol prepared—Baba asked whether he was not Sri Krishna. He told Butty to wait patiently for some time, saying that the idol could be installed afterwards. Nobody could understand the inner meaning of Baba's words. The temple was coming up gradually. Baba made all arrangements personally and if he wanted to tell his devotees about anything, he told them in their dreams.

Khushal Chand of Rahata

One evening Baba asked Kaka Dixit to go to Rahata and fetch Khushal Chand, he had not seen since a long time. When Dixit went to Rahata in a *tonga* to fetch Khushal Chand, he found him already getting ready to come to Shirdi. Khushal Chand told Dixit that Baba had appeared in his dream in the afternoon and asked him to come to Shirdi and therefore he was getting ready. So, both of them started for Shirdi in the tonga brought by Dixit. Khushal Chand was overwhelmed with joy at the way Baba showed his love for him.

Punjabi Ramlal of Bombay

One day Baba appeared in the dream of Ramlal as a saint and asked him to come to him. But Ramlal did not know who this saint was and where to find him. When he was walking along a street in the evening, he saw the photo of Baba in a shop and he was attracted to it like a magnet. He found out that the saint who had appeared in his dream and the person in the photo were one and the same. He went to Shirdi and remained there till his death.

Vijayanand

Vijayanand was a *sanyasi* from Madras. On his way to Mansarovar he stopped at Shirdi and stayed for few days. He ascertained the details about the journey to Mansarovar from Somadeva Swamy who also was at Shirdi. Learning that the pilgrimage would be full of difficulties, he went to Baba and prostrated before him. Baba got angry and told the devotees who were there that they should not befriend this useless *sanyasi* and that he may be driven out.

Having commenced the pilgrimage, to leave it half way finding it difficult was not the quality of an enlightened person. Once having started a work, it should be finished at any cost, facing the difficulties bravely. This is the quality of the courageous. This applies also in spiritual matters. This is the reason why Baba addressed him as a useless *sanyasi.* Even though Baba was angry with him, Vijayanand's love for Baba remained the same. He sat in a corner of the mosque and observed the various activities that took place there.

At the *darbar* (audience session) held in the morning were a large number of devotees. They were worshipping Baba in several ways. Some did *abhishek* to his feet. Some collected the *abhishek* water that dripped from the toe of his leg and drank it. Some touched his feet with their hands and put the hands on their eyes. Some collected in small vessels the water with which his feet were washed, and took them home. Some applied sandalpaste to Baba's neck and hands. Some others sprayed scent on his dress. Some garlanded him while others showered flowers at his feet. In the middle some were giving camphor *arathi.* Now and then Baba adjusted his headgear. He fondled the heads of some devotees and blessed them. He gave a handful of *pedas* (sweets) to the children who came to bow before him. He kept some children on his lap and fed them the sweets personally. Vijayanand, on seeing these things which were taking place, without any feeling of caste, religion, nationality and sex, felt like not leaving Shirdi and stayed on for some time.

One day Vijayanand received a letter informing him that his mother was sick. He met Baba and asked for permission to go home. But as his life's journey was in another direction, Baba declined to give him permission and told him, "Why did you take *sanyas* if your attachment was so much for your mother? Once you take to saffron robe you should not show attachment to any other thing.

This is the importance of the saffron robe. There are a number of thieves in the Wada. Carefully bolt from inside and sleep. Thieves will steal everything wealth, fame and name are not permanent. Because of your noble acts in your previous birth, you could come here. Whoever seeks refuse at the feet of God is relieved of all sufferings and he attains salvation. So without having any desires, do *Parayana* of 'Bhagavatha' in three *saptahas.* God will be satisfied and will remove your sufferings."

Sitting alone in Lendi Bagh as per Baba's orders, Vijayanand did *Parayana* twice and became very tired. On the third day he put his head on the thigh of Bade Baba and expired. Baba having known the last chapter of Vijayanand's life did not allow him to get himself entangled in worldly matters, had detained him at Shirdi and made him read holy books and thus helped him in merging with God.

Madras Bhajan Samaj

In the year 1916, a Bhajan Samaj belonging to Ramadasi system from Madras was on its way to Kashi. On hearing about Sai Baba the members visited Shirdi on their way. The main members of the Samaj were a male, his wife, daughter and sister-in-law. They stayed for a few days at Shirdi and sang good devotional songs and did *bhajan* in the evenings daily. The wife was very devotional and good at heart. But the other three members were always thinking about the presents that Baba would give them. Baba was pleased with the devotion of the wife and at *arathi* time gave her *darshan* as Sri Rama, her preferred God. When she told about this to the other members of the Samaj, they told her that it was only her illusion and made fun of her.

After a few days her husband had a dream which goes as follows: when he was in a big town, the police arrested him. They tied his hands with a rope and put him in a cage. Sai Baba was standing near the cage. Then he told Sai Baba, "On hearing your name and fame we came to your feet.

When you are here in person why this has happened to me?" Baba replied, "You have to suffer for your actions." Then he told Baba, "If I had inadvertently committed any sins in my previous birth, please burn them like hay." Then Baba asked whether he had such confidence in him and he replied that he had full faith in him. Then Baba asked him to close his eyes. When he opened his eyes, he found the policemen lying down bleeding. He was released from the cage. Then Baba told him, "Now you will be caught by the higher officers." Then he prayed to Baba, "Except you there is none to save me. You save me somehow." Baba asked him to close his eyes once again. When he opened them he found himself out of the cage and standing next to Baba. He fell at his feet. Then Baba asked him whether there was any difference between the *namaskar* he had done previously and the 'namaskar' he was doing now. He replied there was a lot of difference. The earlier *namaskar* was done with a desire to get money from Baba. The present *namaskar* was done treating Baba as God and done with devotion. Baba asked him whether he had anymore desires. He told Baba that he had a desire to have the *darshan* of his Guru 'Ramdas'. Baba asked him to turn around and see. When he did, he saw his Guru 'Ramdas' who became invisible after giving him *darshan.* He told Baba that he appeared like an old man. Then Baba said, "Am I old? See now," and asked him to run along with him. Baba ran some distance and became invisible. With this the dream ended and he woke up from his sleep.

He thought over the dream deeply. The cage indicated the desire for money. The 'Dharma' would punish those who were greedy. That was shown as the police. When he developed faith in Baba, the cage opened, which meant that the greed disappeared. Even *dharma* cannot punish those who are not greedy. That was why the police fell down. Baba ran and merged in the universe. He ran behind Baba. This was the human soul following God.

Through this one dream Baba taught him so many matters and made him understand things properly. This is the competence of Sadguru. That morning when he bowed in salutation before Baba, he blessed him and gave him two rupees and sweets and said, "Allah will do you good," and that he would get a lot of money. As per Baba's blessings their pilgrimage went off well and they got a lot of money. They sang in praise of Shirdi Sai Baba at many places. Even after reaching home they propogated much about Baba.

Baba "Crossing the Border" (Seemollanghan)

It was October 1916. The day was *Vijayadasami* (Dushera festival). As per the tradition, all the villagers would go up to the boundary of the village in a procession, cross the boundary and come back. This was called "Seemollanghan" or crossing the border. On that day also when they returned after "Seemollanghan", Baba suddenly became angry, his eyes became red like balls of fire and his body temperature rose. He removed all the items of dress on his body including his headgear, tore them and threw them into the Dhuni. Because of this, the flames in the Dhuni rose high. Baba's naked body was shining bright due to the reflection of the flames. His two eyes looked like two bright lamps. All the villagers gathered near Dwarakamai to witness this strange scene. Baba, turning towards, them thundered, "Look at me carefully and say whether I am a Hindu or a Muslim." Everyone began shivering at his sudden outburst. None had the courage to open his mouth. There was complete silence for some moments. Then Bhagoji Shinde went to Baba and tried to tie a fresh 'Langota' (a loincloth) and found the body temperature so hot he could not touch it with his hand. Anyhow he tied the 'langota' and asked Baba why he was doing all this on the day of 'Seemollanghan'. Baba again thundered, "Today is my Seemollanghan." So saying, he hit the floor with his *sataka* with force. Bhagoji next dressed up Baba with a long shirt and made him sit. Tatya came and applied sandalpaste all over the body. Baba did not cool down till ten in the night. Finally he calmed down and was ready for the Chavadi procession. Bhagoji touched Baba's right hand once, while he was walking and found it soft and cold. None understood Baba's words when he said, "Today is my Seemollanghan." But he indicated that exactly two years from this day he would be crossing his life's border. After his *Samadhi* on Dushera day in the year 1918, everyone understood Baba's statement.

In spite of reading many holy books, hearing many good lectures and moving in good company it is very difficult to put into practice, the good things we learn. This is human weakness. Let us pray to Sai Baba for Seemollanghan of this weaknesses in our readers.

Om Shanti ! Shanti ! Shantihi !

CHAPTER 29

Balaram Mankar

Balaram Mankar became dejected after the death of his wife, handing over the household responsibility to his son, he came to Shirdi and remained there with Baba. His devotion was appreciated by Baba.

Once Sai Baba gave him Rs.12 and asked him to go to Machindragarh and stay there, meditating thrice a day. After experiencing the natural beauty, pure drinking water and healthy air, Mankar felt happy and meditated regularly as directed by Baba.

One day Baba gave him *darshan* while he was in conscious state. He asked Baba why he was sent to that place. Baba replied, "While at Shirdi so many thoughts were in your mind and hence to make your mind stable, I sent you here. You imagined me as a person made of five elements and three and a half cubits in length. You also thought that I am always at Shirdi. Now say whether the Baba you see here and the Baba you saw at Shirdi are the same or not. I have sent you here only to prove this."

After sometime Mankar started for Bandra and wanted to travel from Poona to Dadar by train. When he went to purchase the ticket he found the booking office crowded with people buying tickets. He could not get a ticket. Then a villager with a blanket over him, approached Mankar and enquired where he wanted to go. When Mankar told him it was Dadar, the villager gave him a ticket to Dadar saying that he had cancelled his visit due to some other work. Mankar lowered his head to look at the ticket and by the time he lifted his head the villager was not to be seen. He waited for him till the departure time of the train but could not find him. He went home and again came to Shirdi and remained with Baba till his last days. He was very lucky to have died in Shirdi.

Completion of the Temple Construction by Butty

Butty, with the intention of completing the construction of the Krishna temple early, was getting things done quickly. Shama was regularly supervising the construction work, while Bapu Saheb Jog, Tatya, Ramachander Patil and other devotees were helping him in this work. With Baba's grace the construction of Butty Wada was completed in December, 1916. Some minor items like carvings, polishing, etc., remained.

Waman Narvekar

Waman Narvekar was the devotee who loved Baba wholeheartedly. Once he brought a rupee with him. On the obverse were the images of Sita, Rama and Lakshman and on the reverse side was the image of the Reverent Anjaneya (Hanuman). He gave the coin to Baba. His desire was to have the coin consecrated by Baba and to keep it in his house for worship. But Baba put it in his pocket. Shama, knowing the desire of Narvekar, requested Baba to return the coin to Narvekar. Baba asked why he should return the coin and wanted to keep it with him. But, if Narvekar gave Rs.25, then the coin would be returned to him. As Narvekar did not have the money with him, he borrowed from others and gave this to Baba. Then Baba said, "This coin is valued more than Rs.25, Shama. Let us keep the coin with us. Keep it in your puja room and worship it." No one had the courage to ask Baba about his action. Perhaps, Baba did it for the good of Narvekar.

Ramchander Patil

Ramchander Patil was a friend and relative of Tatya Kote Patil. Having known the greatness of Baba, he also worshipped Baba daily with devotion and sincerity. He and Tatya used to do service together during the Chavadi procession and also while Baba was in Lendi Bagh. At the end of December 1916 he fell seriously ill. In spite of using several medicines there was no relief. Unable to take food and water properly, he became week and bedridden. He became discouraged. He lost hope of survival and thought that death was imminent.

One night he prayed to Baba to give him early death so that he could these sufferings. That night Baba appeared at his bedside. Ramachander Patil wept and told Baba that he could not suffer like this any longer and requested him to help him in dying early. Sai Baba, the Love Incarnation, asked him not to fear as he (Baba) had removed his death slip and that he would recover soon. But he expressed his concern to Ramachander about the impending death of Tatya, who would die on the Vijayadasami day in 1918. He asked Ramachander not to reveal this to anyone, including Tatya, for if Tatya came to know, he would fear.

Ramachander Patil knew that Baba's words would never fail. He became healthy soon. But he was always worried about Tatya, and unable to keep the secret he told Bala Shimpe. Since Tatya was a friend of both they began to worry a lot about Tatya.

Time was passing by. The year 1916 came to an end and the new year began. Butty was very anxious to get Sri Krishna's idol installed in the Butty Wada which was built at a huge cost. Whenever he asked Baba for permission to order for Sri Krishna's idol, Baba asked him to have patience and wait. The number of devotees who were visiting Baba increased enormously. Sai Baba's greatness and *leelas* spread to the four sides of our country.

Baba's Holi Meal in Hemadpant's House

On Holi festival in 1917, Baba appeared in the dream of Hemadpant at his house in Bandra and told him that he would be coming to his house to participate in the Holi meal. Hemadpant told his wife about the dream and asked her to prepare food for one more person. The festivities of Holi were over. Arrangements were made for serving the meal. They reserved a seat for Baba. All the members of the family sat down for the meal. After offerings were made to God, ghee was served; they were about to start eating. When someone knocked at the door. Hemadpant opened the door and found two persons standing there. They handed over to him a photo of Shirdi Sai Baba with a request to keep it safely. They asked him to finish his meals first and then they could discuss the details about the photo later on; they left the place.

Hemadpant was surprised at the arrival of Baba in the form of photo, exactly at meal time. He shed tears of joy. He felt happy that what Baba had told him in the dream had come true in this manner. He immediately put the photo in the place set apart for Baba. All the food items were kept before the photo and only after offering them to Baba, did the others eat.

The same day at the same time Baba told Shama at Shirdi that he had a sumptuous meal at Bandra in Hemadpant's house. Shama could understand Baba's words only after sometime when Hemadpant went to Shirdi. Now let us see how the photo was delivered at Hemadpant's house.

A long time back, a saint by name Abdul Rehman gave a lifesize framed photo of Baba to Ali Mohammed. After sometime, Ali's brother-in-law fell sick. Someone said that if the photos of saints were put in the sea, the illness would subside. So he sent for his manager and asked him to collect all such photos in his house and also in the houses of relatives and put them in the sea. After some days Ali Mohammed came home and was surprised to find that Baba's photo was still there on the wall. He began to think to whom it should be given. As per Baba's order given to him through his thoughts, the photo was handed over to Hemadpant.

Lala Laxmichand

Lala Laxmichand heard for the first time about Baba in the year 1910, through the Hari Kathas rendered by Das Ganu. After that he saw him in his dream. He was very eager to go to Shirdi and see him. While this was so, his friend Shankar Rao came to him and told him that he was going to Shirdi and asked him to accompany him. Laxmichand was very much pleased. He borrowed sixteen rupees and made arrangements for his journey. Both of them did *bhajan* (singing of devotional song) in the train. They thought of taking some guavas for Baba. Coinciding with their thoughts, an old woman came with a basket of guavas. They purchased some, and the old woman asked them to take the remaining fruits also along with them to Shirdi and present them to Baba on her behalf.

Laxmichand prostrated before Baba and the moment he touched his feet, his heart melted. Baba said, "Cunning person! He did *bhajan* on his way. What is the use of asking others about me? Has his desire been fulfilled? Where was the need to borrow sixteen rupees and come for my *darshan*? "Realising that what Baba said was about him he was surprised at his omniscience.

Laxmichand liked *sanja* (a wheat preparation). One day no one had brought *sanja.* But Baba ordered Bapu Saheb Jog to get prepare two pots full of *sanja.* He asked Laxmichand to take whatever quantity of it he could eat. Laxmichand was surprised that Baba knew about his favourite food and got it prepared, which proves that there is nothing in this world that Baba did not know. He reposed complete faith in Baba for the rest of his life.

Shrimati Mehta—The Burhanpore Lady

Smt. Mehta was resident of Burhanpore. Baba once appeared in her dream and wanted *khichidi* (rice cooked with dal). She tried her best to prepare it and offer it to Baba, but an opportune time had not come for a long time. At last in the month of April 1917, she went along with her husband to Shirdi. There also she could not prepare *khichdi* for fifteen days. But one day with determination, she procured the necessary foodstuff and prepared it. She went with it to the mosque at about noon. A curtain was drawn across the entrance which was an indication that none should enter inside the mosque. Though she knew of this practice, she could not wait further and in the eagerness to serve Baba *khichidi,* she went inside and put the plate before him. Baba ate it eagerly and quickly. All those who were there were surprised. She also lost herself in joy on seeing Baba's enjoyment. How anxious she had been for so many years to serve Baba with *khichidi;* now with the same anxiousness Baba had accepted it. Everyone was happy at the extraordinary love of Baba towards his devotees.

God's Treasury

One day Baba narrated a story which might have taken place in one of his previous incarnations. "In my younger days, I had been to Beedgaon in search of livelihood. There I secured a job in a factory manufacturing knitted cloth. I used to work very hard. The proprietor was satisfied with my work. There were three workers before me. The first worker was paid Rs.50, the second worker was paid Rs.100 and third worker Rs.150. But I was paid double the money of all the three amounts put together—Rs.600. The proprietor appreciated my work and loved me. I did the work given to me with devotion. Hence I used to think that the salary I was getting was given by God and carefully saved it. What is given by a human will not last long. But what God has given will remain permanently. My God Allah asks the devotees to take as much as they want. But the devotees come to me and ask me to give. If a thing is given once, it is not sufficient. The number of devotees who want everything everytime has increased. There is none to understand what I am saying. My God's Treasury is full and overflowing. Any real devotee can take away cartloads from this. But none is interested in it. My fakir's tact and my divine acts are extraordinary. My body will join the earth and my breath will join the air. As long as there is life in me, this opportunity is there. I go somewhere and will do some work. But this *Maya* is troubling me. In spite of all these difficulties, I am anxious about my devotees. I am ever alert in the case of them. The reward I give them depends on their effort. Those who believe in me and those who never forget me will have endless joy."

Bala Buva Sutar

One evening, Baba on his way to Lendi Bagh stopped for a few seconds before Butty Wada. Bala Buva Sutar, a *yogi* from Bombay who came to Shirdi for the first time, saluted Baba. Blessing him with raised hand, Baba said that he knew him since four years. Bala Buva Sutar was surprised. He thought over the matter deeply and recollected having saluted Baba's photo at Bombay, four years back. He was surprised at Baba's omniscience.

Hari Bavu Karnik

Karnik came to Shirdi on Guru Poornima day in 1917. He worshipped Baba and gave him clothes and *dakshina.* While he was going down the steps of the mosque, he thought of giving one more rupee as *dakshina.* As there was a convention that one should not go back to see Baba after taking leave of him, he started his journey back home. On the way he visited the temple of Kala Ram in Nashik. While he was coming out a *yogi* named Narasingh Maharaj, who was talking with his disciples, left them and came to Hari Bavu, and catching hold of his hand firmly, said, "Give me my one rupee." Hari Bavu was surprised that Sai Baba was taking a rupee through this *yogi* and gave the coin to him. All *yogis* are one. All Gods are one. In fact, there is no, difference between *yogis* and *Gods.* Thus, Baba collected the amounts which devotees had vowed to offer other Gods but forgot to fulfil their vows.

Taking Leave of Baba

From 1905 to 1917 many devotees from distant places came to Shirdi and remained there for a long time, experiencing Baba's love. Those who had lived with jealousy, selfishness, hatred, ego and attachments and then experienced Sai's love, were not inclined to leave Shirdi. But Baba used to send back some of them, as they had to discharge their duties towards their families. They would start their journey back home, as per Baba's orders, but after going some distance, unable to bear the separation from Baba, they would weep and remain in Shirdi village till dusk; they would go back to Baba in the night, as he would not ask them to leave Shirdi at night time. Noticing this weakness in the devotees, Baba strictly ordered that once the devotees took leave of him to go back to their homes, they should not return. If anyone came back, he would face a lot of difficulties in his journey. This rule was intended only to make the devotees disciplined.

Let us resolve to always remember the things we learn from the stories in the *Life History of Sai Baba* and see him in our hearts every moment. Let us pray to Sai Baba to give us strength, not to go back on our resolve, in the same manner as the devotees who had once taken leave of Baba, should not return back.

Om Shanti ! Shanti ! Shantihi !

CHAPTER 30

It was the year 1917. Devotees kept coming to Shirdi in very large numbers like ants. A good number were drawn to Shirdi by Baba in the same manner as a thread is tied to the leg of a sparrow and drawn. The following is the story of one such devotee.

Appa Saheb Kulkarni

One day a fakir resembling Baba came to Kulkarni's house at about noon. Kulkarni was not in the house. His wife and children asked the *fakir* whether he was Shirdi Sai Baba. The *fakir* replied that he was a servant of God and on His orders only he came to enquire about the welfare of Kulkarni's family. He asked for *dakshina.* Kulkarni's wife gave him a rupee. The *fakir* gave her some *udi* and asked her to keep it in her *puja* for worship. That evening when Kulkarni returned home and heard of the *fakir's* visit, he felt sorry for not being present at then. He told his family that he would have given ten rupees *dakshina.* Though he was hungry, he went out in search of the *fakir.* As he could not find him anywhere, he returned home, had his meal and again started along with a friend in search of the *fakir.* All of a sudden the *fakir* came from behind and extending his hand asked for the *dakshina.* Kulkarni gave him a rupee. Again the *fakir* asked *dakshina* and he gave him one more rupee. When the *fakir* asked again he took three rupees from his friend and gave to it to the *fakir.* As he found the *fakir* not fully satisfied, he took him home and gave him another four rupees. When the *fakir* asked again, he gave him a ten-rupee note. The *fakir* gave him back nine rupees and went away. Since Kulkarni wanted to give ten rupees as *dakshina,* the *fakir* was not satisfied till he got the ten rupees. Kulkarni kept the nine rupees consecrated given back to him by the *fakir* in his *puja* room and worshipped them. When once Kulkarni visited Shirdi, he got a strand of Baba's hair. He put it in a small silver container and tied it to his hand. After those two incidents, he got a lot of money and also progressed much spiritually.

It was the talk of those days that Sai Baba's hand was without bones and he would never send away anyone who approached him empty-handed. Because of this, many people like singers, astrologers and street circus performers came to Baba and exhibited their talents and received presents. When close devotees of Baba visited him along with their family members, Baba gave them clothes. Other than accepting *dakshina,* Baba never associated himself with any other financial matters. If someone came to Baba with any such proposals, he told them frankly that he did not want to involve himself in such affairs.

Baba not only never yielded to the lure of the lucre but also followed the same principle in respect of ladies. He was an *Askalika Brahmachari* throughout.

Sai Appearing as a Snake

Raghu Patil, a resident of Shirdi village, would start any work, only after visiting Baba and saluting him. Once, he went to Nevasa village to see his brother-in-law. He went by horse up to Srirampur and from there by tonga to Nevasa. He woke up the next morning and remembered Baba, praying to him with closed eyes. He heard the following words in Baba's voice, "If I give *darshan,* do not be frightened." In the meanwhile a servant working in the cowshed cried, "Snake! Snake!" All ran there. Raghu Patil thought that Sai had come in that form and put a bowl containing milk in front of the snake, and it drank the milk. The frightened people ran away. While Raghu Patil was watching, the snake crawled for some distance and disappeared. He felt very happy that Sai had given him *darshan* in the form of a snake.

Feeding Baba

Among the women devotees who served Baba with utmost devotion were Baija Bai, Radhakrishna Mai and Lakshmi Bai Shinde. After the demise of Radhakrishna Mai, Lakshmi Bai Shinde attended personally to the needs of Sai Baba, like a daughter serving her father. In those days she was the richest women in Shirdi village having an exemplary character and serving Baba day and night. In the nights, only Mhalsapathi, Tatya and Lakshmi Bai were permitted into the mosque.

One evening, in 1917, when Baba and Tatya were conversing in the mosque, Lakshmi Bai came and saluted Baba. Baba told her that he was hungry. She told him that she would go home and bring food for him. After a short while, she brought roti (leavened bread) and curry. Baba took the food and threw it to the dog which was there. The dog ate the food completely and was wagged its tail out of joy. Then Lakshmi Bai asked Baba why he had given her the trouble to prepare the food, when he did not eat it, but gave it to the dog. Baba replied "Please do not feel for it. To satisfy the hunger of the dog is the same as satisfying my hunger. Animals also have *Atma.* Lives may be different but hunger is the same. Humans can speak but animals cannot. Whoever satisfies the hungry will be giving me complete satisfaction. Know this as a great truth." From what Sai said we learn that he is present in all living beings, Omnipresent, and Immortal. Let us will recollect what Baba said in such matters, "You need not go to distant places in search of me. If you cast aside your name and body form, *Atma* remains. This is there in all living beings. I am the *Atma.* If you can carefully realise this truth, you will know my true form and merge in me."

Bapu Saheb Jog's Sanyas

After retirement from service in 1909, Bapu Saheb Jog came to Shirdi along with his wife and settled there permanently.

They had no children and therefore no family responsibilities. Both of them were completely immersed in the service of Baba. After the death of Megha, Jog gave *arathis* in the mosque and Chavadi. He did this only till Baba's *Samadhi.* He was also called Pujari Jog. In the evenings, he would recite sacred books like the *Jnaneshwari* and *Eknath Baghavata* and explain them to the devotees who assembled there. But he did not enjoy peace of mind in spite of doing all these.

One day he asked Baba, "Baba, I am fully immersed in your service since so long. But there is no peace of mind for me. Why? When are you going to take pity on me?" Baba replied, "Wait for some more time. The sufferings for your past actions will be over. Your merits and de-merits will be burnt down to ashes. When you renounce all your attachments, conquer your lust and sense of tastes, and overcome all other obstacles, then your life will be a blessed one." After sometime his wife died. As there was no other attachment for him he took *sanyas.* We must carefully observe Baba's message in the above story. After overcoming our weaknesses like jealousy, selfishness and hatred, the other small enemies like, attachment, lust and tastes will remain and unless we win over these also, there will not be complete peace. The Sadguru teaches such things to his disciples according to their levels, and takes them on the *Jnana Marga.* But some Gurus who take the status and wealth of the disciples into consideration, cannot understand the level of the disciples. Even suppose such a Guru understands the level of his disciples to a certain extent, he will not teach them the main things for fear that they may leave him. This is the difference between Shirdi Sai Baba and the numerous Gurus that exist nowadays.

Arrival of Bal Gangadhar Tilak at Shirdi

Khaparde came along with Bal Gangadhar Tilak, to Shirdi on 19 May 1917. Khaparde who had come earlier also to Shirdi, had seen the greatness of Baba personally. Hence he brought Tilak who was the extremist leader in the Indian National Congress and a freedom fighter, to have *darshan* of Baba and take his advice in the matter of freedom movement. There were proofs that Baba gave Tilak certain advices secretly. According to the then prevailing conditions under British rule, these matters were kept secret. After Tilak left Shirdi, then District Collector of Ahmednagar sent a CID Officer to Shirdi to keep an eye on the activities of Sai Baba and send a confidential report.

There were several proofs to show that Baba predicted that India would certainly become an independent nation, through a non-violent revolution only and not through extremist violent acts. He gave advice to Tilak along the above lines and there were indications that from that day the extremist actions were toned down.

Hindu-Muslim Unity

In those days, to attain independence for our country was the main issue. This was a political problem. The main social problem in the country was religious differences between Hindus and Muslims. The British Government did not try wholeheartedly to remove these differences. On the other hand, they encouraged such differences. They thought that the minds of the people could be diverted from the movement for independence, if the religious differences were encouraged. Religious clashes occurred in the predominantly Muslim populated areas of Aurangabad and nearby places causing much hardship to the ordinary citizen. Unrest, disputes, loss of lives and properties were plaguing the society. Baba found that communal harmony could bring peace and happiness to the people rather than rituals. He also found that in both the religions and religious leaders, the qualities of equality, cooperation and love were completely absent. There was none then to bring peace to the commonman in the fields of religion and politics. That was why Sai Baba dedicated himself to the cause of Hindu-Muslim unity and reminded all, that God is one *Sab ka Malik ek hai.* The truths in both the religions were same. The gist of the two religions was the same. But the trouble lay with the heads of these two religions and their blind beliefs. The movement started by Baba for Hindu-Muslim unity was found to be necessary for the country's political future and hence Mahatma Gandhi gave the slogan "Hindu-Muslim Bhai Bhai". The main aim in Sai's philosophy was to unite all religions. That was why he resided in a mosque where he started the Dhuni which was sacred to the Hindus. In the front side of the mosque he planted a tulasi plant. The slogans given at the end of arthis Sai Nath Maharaj Ki Jai etc., resemble those recited at the end of the 'namaz' by the Muslims, and were prescribed by Sai Baba. In this manner Shirdi Sai Baba made sincere efforts to unite both the religions.

Before trying to understand Baba's conception of communal harmony, let us try to know what is religion and how it came into being. Religion was only a set of norms prescribed for the people living in different parts of the world, for their ways of living in relation to their societies. The humans established a society for smooth living, different from non-humans like animals, etc. When different kinds of people lived together in a society, there would naturally be a clash of behaviours resulting in suffering to some. The living methods were decided keeping in view the climatic conditions of that place and the availability of natural resources. Taking into consideration all these aspects, certain experienced people had indicated certain norms to be followed. Some meant for the self and some for his behaviour in a society without causing difficulties to others. In this manner the social regulations and taboos came into existence and developed into religions. So, religion means the regulated behaviour and actions of the people in a society. The aim was to see that all sections of people in a society were happy.

As time passed, such religions developed hatred among societies, leading to bloodshed. The causes for this were not religions or the philosophies but the religious leaders. We had seen in the story of the 'Two Goats' in chapter 18 that two brothers born to the same mother and belonging to the same religion killed each other. Same blood and same religion could not prevent this. Therefore, there is nothing wrong with religion and if at all there is something, it is only in the people. We should put an end to the hatred towards other religions. Our hearts should be filled with tolerance and love for other religions and equal treatment meted out to people of different religions. This is the philosophy of Sai Baba towards religious harmony. If we look at our country today, with a name like Hindustan, it has a number of people belonging to other religions—Muslims, Christians, Sikhs and Jains. Now and then, in the name of religions, atrocities are being committed. The cause for this is not religion but religious leaders. Because of so many religions, India has been declared as a secular country.

If so many religions are there in a country differences between the religions are bound to be there. Hence, some intellectuals are of the opinion that it would be good to have only one religion in a country. This appears to be a good proposal but it is important to know the methods by which it can be achieved. Violent methods should not be used. We must proceed only in the path shown by Sai Baba—*Prema Marga.* Marriages between persons belonging to two different religions should be encouraged. In this ways all religions can be intermixed to establish a Sai Religion by which we can forget all religious differences. The politicians and religious heads may take an initiative in this matter, so that there will not be any opposition form others.

Let us pray to Sai Baba that in this Sai Yuga the Sai Religion spreads not only in our country but throughout this world.

Om Shanti ! Shanti ! Shantihi !

End of Sixth Day's Parayan

SEVENTH DAY'S 'PARAYANA'— WEDNESDAY

CHAPTER 31

Bala Shimpe was doing tailoring work in Shirdi. Tatya got Baba's clothes stitched by him. Now and then devotees from Bombay and Poona brought long coats and presented them to Baba. For the satisfaction of the devotees Baba kept the clothes with him for a few days and later on gave them away to devotees who were dependent on him. Some sent big shoes, chillum pipes, *satakas* and sweets from different places. Whenever sweets were offered by the devotees in large quantities, Baba called the village children and making them sit on his lap, offered them sweets. These children who sat on Baba's lap were very lucky!

The following facts about Sai Baba spread through the length and breadth of Maharashtra just like the smell of scent spreading through air.

i) If one steps into Shirdi, all the sufferings will disappear.
ii) If one steps into the mosque (Dwarakamai) one will have happiness and wealth.
iii) Whatever words come out of Baba's mouth, will prove true and
iv) By touching Baba's feet one's desires will be fulfilled.

Several devotees came and worshipped Sai Baba and sought only materialistic benefits. Though they were taught in several ways by Baba that their desires were temporary, again their minds got entangled in worldly objects. Shirdi Sai Baba who was the incarnation of God was pained at the desires of the devotees. Noticing the day-to-day increase in the number of such devotees, he said, "I have been seeing since a long time. All are thieves. I have to move with such persons. I am struggling day and night to set right such persons. I am also praying to Allah in this matter. But Allah is not accepting my prayer. Whether I am alive or not my prayer will be accepted. I will not pray for others. The people are generally not of good behaviour. They are not gentle. They are fickle minded. Very few have shown interest in spiritual matters and spiritual practices. People are becoming mean-minded and causing me pain. Always they are pestering me for materialistic benefits." This way Baba indicated in the beginning of the year 1918, that it had become imperative to end his *Avatar.*

Sai Baba frequently used the Arabic word "Allah Malik". If any of the devotees referred to him as a great person, Baba told, "God is the greatest of all. He is the Master of all. None equals God. Just imagine how powerful is God who has created this Universe, sustaining it and finally merging it in Him. Such a powerful God had given us certain stages in this birth, and we should be content with that and be happy. How God wanted us to be, we will be and whatever pleasures and sufferings He gives us, we shall be content with that. Only God has full freedom. All the human beings should work with a feeling that they are acting as per the orders of God and offer their all to Him without caring for loss or gain. Only then will we get salvation, or moksha. On the other hand, if we go against God's orders due to nescience *(ajnana)* and delusion *(moha)* we have to take several births to wipe off these actions. *Jnana* is the way to attain *moksha*, and *ajnana* will lead us to the cycle of death and re-birth. Therefore, we must obtain *Jnana* from Sadguru, and get over the cycle of death and re-birth and desire no other thing from him." Thus Sai Baba himself told us what to ask and what not to ask from Him.

In the same manner Sai Baba told several times how our behaviour should be in this world, "Never hate anyone. Do not quarrel with anyone. Love all living beings. Do not have revengeful attitude. Do not insult anyone. If anyone talks about you in harsh words, get away from there without getting offended. Then their harsh words will not affect you. Avoid laziness. Always be doing good work. If there is no work to do, read holy books or repeat God's name *(Namasmaran).* Do not develop hatred or jealousy for others. Children should obey their parents. They should assist their parents in work. They should always speak only the truth. If someone talks to us in ten words, we should reply in one word, that is easily understandable. Do not have a tit-for-tat attitude. Do good to those who did bad to you."

For those on the spiritual path, Baba advised as follows, "Eat little. Sleep less. Do not go after several tastes of food. Be content with one or two tastes. Do not indulge in finding faults in others and cruelty to living things. For self-realisation, meditation is important. Meditation keeps the mind in peace. The peaceful mind will attain the state of *Samadhi* (spiritual superconsciousness). Unless you discard your desires, it is not possible to meditate by keeping the mind stable. Without attachment in the previous birth, none will come to you. Therefore do not drive away any living being that comes to you."

In this manner Baba advised his devotees. With *arathis* three times a day and with a large number of devotees attending, Dwarakamai wore a festive look every day. Butty was anxious to install Sree Krishna's idol in the Wada built by him. As he did not have the courage to ask Baba for his permission, he kept his desire in his heart. Ramachander Patil and Bala Shimpe were fearing the impending death of Tatya. Nana Chandorkar, whenever he got an opportunity, was explaining the greatness of Baba to the people. Das Ganu through his Hari Kathas was spreading Baba's *leelas* in the entire Maharashtra. Bapu Saheb Jog was serving Baba by giving *arathis* regularly every day. Close devotees like Mhalsapathi were enjoying the love of Baba to their heart's content by way of his *darshan,* touch and nectar-like words. Thousands of devotees came to Shirdi, worshipped Baba, and had their desires fulfilled. Tatya who was not aware of his impending death, was serving Baba with a pure heart like a lotus flower floating on the surface of the water. In this manner, Baba had already decided as to the duties of each devotee and all was going on well.

Anand Rao's Dream Vision

According to Baba's orders, Kaka Saheb Dixit was reading Bhavardha Ramayan daily and explaining it to the others. One day he was explaining about the Nava Nathas' elucidation of the characteristics of devotees, contained in the eleventh Skandha of the second chapter of the book. The substance of all the exposition of the Nava Nathas was that in this age of Kali, the only means of liberation was the remembrance of Hari's (Lord's) or Guru's feet. After reading this, Kaka Saheb entertained a doubt as to how to reach the devotional path indicated by the Nava Nathas, saying that it would be difficult to put that into practice. Shama did not agree with the thinking of Kaka Saheb and argued that their devotion to Baba was no less than that expounded by the Nava Nathas. The same night Anandrao Pakhde, who had partaken in the above discussions, had a dream, in which Baba gave him the following vision, as narrated by Anandrao Pakhde: "I was standing waist-deep in a very deep sea and I saw Sai Baba all of a sudden. He was sitting on a gold throne studded with diamonds. His feet were in the water. The vision was like a real one, very unlike a dream. Shama was there by the side of me. He asked me to fall at Baba's feet. I asked him how it was possible since Baba's feet were below the water. Then Shama requested Baba to raise his feet above the water and Baba did so. Then I put my head on his feet. Baba blessed me and told me that I would benefit by this and should not have anxiety and fear. Baba asked me to present a silk *dhoti* to Shama."

By saying that Baba's feet were inside water, the actual meaning is that due to an unstable mind, we are unable to see our Guru's feet. By moving in the company of devotees whose minds are stable, one can get a Guru and that was the real meaning of Shama requesting Baba to raise his feet above the water. By asking Anandarao to present a silk *dhoti* to Shama, he meant that one would benefit by serving a devotee who had complete faith in the Guru. As per Baba's order in the vision, Anandrao bought a silk *dhoti* and requested Kaka Saheb to give it to Shama. As Shama did not accept it, they put two slips near Baba's *padukas,* one had the words "accept" and the other "do not accept" written on them. When one of the slips was picked up it contained the word "accept". Then Shama accepted it.

Tilak's Secrets of the *Gita*

Baba encouraged devotees who read holy books and *Brahmavidya* (Metaphysics). One day Bapu Saheb Jog received a book by post. He came to Baba to have his *darshan* and when he bent before him in salutation, the book fell from his armpit. Baba asked for it and turned a few pages. It was the book titled *Gita Rahasya* (Secrets of Gita) written by Tilak. Baba took out a rupee from his pocket and put it on the book and returned the book along with the coin to Jog with an advice to read it carefully and completely which will benefit him. Because Baba had consecrated the book by his touch, Jog benefited a lot from *Parayana* of the book.

Killing of Poisionous Creatures—Baba's Opinion

One day Dixit and his friends were talking on the first floor of Dixit Wada. A snake entered through the window. When an attempt was made to kill it with sticks, it went away. While one devotee Muktaram opined that it was good that the snake went away, Hemadpant differed and said it was good to kill poisonous snakes. The whole day both of them argued over this and finally they asked Baba about it. Baba replied, "God only is the preserver of this entire universe which includes poisonous creatures like scorpions, snakes, etc. Without His permission no harm can come to anyone from them. None of the living beings in this world have any freedom of action. So we should take pity and love all creatures and abstain ourselves from quarrels, killings, etc. God is the protector of all."

Haji Siddique Phalke

As prescribed by his religion, Phalke undertook a pilgrimage to Mecca and Medina and returned. Hearing about Baba, he came to Shirdi. But Baba did not allow him to enter the mosque for nine months. He felt discouraged and approched Shama. On behalf of the Haji, Shama intervened and asked, "Baba, You have blessed many who have come to you. But why you are not blessing the old Haji?" Then Baba replied, "What can I do when Allah is not agreeing? Without his permission none can enter the mosque. You go to the Haji and find out whether he could come near the Bharavi Well." Shama went and found out that he was prepared to come there. Baba asked Shama to find out from the Haji whether he was prepared to pay Rs.4000 in four instalments. Shama asked Haji and found out that he was even prepared to pay the sum. Baba again asked Shama to tell the Haji that a goat would be cut in the mosque and whether he wanted its meat or its testicles. Shama got the reply from the Haji that he would be satisfied with a small piece of meat from Baba's mud pot. Hearing these answers Baba got angry. He went to Chavadi where the Haji was staying and said to him, "Why are you acting like a great man? You are feeling proud of your pilgrimage to Mecca and failed to know who I am." Afterwards Baba took him into his durbar. The condition that the Haji should come to Bharavi Well was a test for the Haji's egoism. If the Haji would have refused to go to the Bharavi Well, it would indicate his egoism. By asking money, Baba tested his sacrificial quality. By asking whether the Haji wanted meat or the testicles, the sensory tastes were known. After testing the Haji in the three qualities, Baba took him into his durbar.

Abdul Baba (Bade Baba)

Abdul was a resident of Nanded. From his sixteenth year he was serving Fakir Amiruddin, a saint of Nanded. In the year 1889, Baba appeared in a dream of Amiruddin, put two mangoes in his hands and asked him to send Abdul to him. When Amiruddin woke up he really found two mangoes in his hands. He gave them to Abdul, and asked him to go to Shirdi and be in the service of Sai Baba. Abdul came immediately to Shirdi. On seeing him, Baba said that his crow had come. Baba asked him to do his service without any other thoughts. From then onwards Abdul kept the mosque and it's adjoining places clean and also the paths on which Baba walked. He cleaned the lanterns in the mosque, not forgetting Lendi Bagh. In his leisure time he sat near Baba and read the *Quran.* He put two big pots of water near the Nanda Deep in Lendi Bagh. Baba set in the evenings daily at a fixed time near Nanda Deep. He took water in his hands from the pots and reading something sprinkled the water on all sides. After that he got up and looked seriously in all the directions in which water was sprinkled. The devotees used to think that by his actions, Baba was protecting his devotees who were there on all sides. One whole night Abdul knelt down and put his hands on his head and Baba asked him whether he wanted to see the moon. After remaining in that position for sometime, Abdul fell on Baba sleepy. Baba woke him up and told him that he would show him the moon. Next day afternoon, when Abdul took water in his hands, he found the image of the moon in the water.

Abdul washed the clothes of Baba daily in the nearby rivulet and kept them neat.

Imam Bai Chotekhan

Imam Bai Chotekhan was a sepoy in the government of Nizam. Once he severely beat a Christian teacher for having not cooperated in an investigation. The teacher vomitted blood and became unconscious as a result of the beatings. The sepoy's superiors advised him to leave the job and get out of the state to escape punishment. Therefore, he resigned his job and came over to Maharashtra State with the intention of escape the punishment, with the blessings of Shirdi Sai Baba.

When he went to see Baba the next day, Baba assured him saying, "Allah Malik! Do not fear. I will see that no punishment is given to you." He stayed at Shirdi for two months. One day Baba told him, "You can go home. The pending litigations about your lands will be settled in your favour." He had disputes about some lands with his aunt. Though he had not told Baba about this, Baba knew about it and blessed him. Afterwards Chotekhan visited Shirdi several times and took blessings and advice of Baba and progressed in his life.

Butty's Life in Danger

Once an astrologer named Nana Saheb Dengale came to Shirdi. He told Butty one day that the particular day was inauspicious for him and there was dangerous to his life. Butty came to Baba and sat at his feet. Baba asked Butty, "What is, this Nana telling you? He is telling that there is danger to your life. I will see how death will kill you. You do not fear." That evening when Butty went to answer nature's call he found there a big snake. Butty called his servant, and by the time the servant came with a stick, the snake had disappeared. He recollected Baba's assurance and felt happy. Actually that day the poisonous snake might have bitten him as per the prediction of the astrologer, but it could not do anything because of Baba's words and went away.

Ameer Shakkar

Ameer Shakkar was a butcher by caste and belonged to the village Korale near Shirdi. He was doing commission business at Bandra. He suffered from rheumatic pains. Hearing about the greatness of Baba, he left his business and came to Baba. Baba asked him to sit in the Chavadi. In those days the flooring of the Chavadi was damp. Such a flooring was not suitable for a person suffering from asthma. But none can go against Baba's words. So he sat in the Chavadi. Baba used to go to the Chavadi in the mornings and evenings. On alternate days, he used to sleep in the Chavadi. Because of this Ameer cultivated a closeness to Baba. His ailment was slowly getting cured.

One night he went to Kopargaon without informing anyone and stayed in a choultry there. There a fakir was about to die and asked for water. Ameer gave him water and the fakir drank a little and died. Fearing that the police may question him regarding the fakir's death, and regretting for having come without Baba's permission which had resulted in this situation, he immediately returned to Shirdi, chanting Baba's name. He stayed in the Chavadi as per Baba's orders and got cured completely.

One night when Baba was sleeping in the Chavadi, he woke up Abdul in the middle of the night and said that some dangerous creature was coming towards his bed. When Abdul brought the lantern and searched, he found a snake under the pillow of Ameer Shakkar. Baba indicated his own name instead of Ameer's. This way Baba saved Ameer. Let us pray to Baba to similarly protect the readers of his *Life History*.

Om Shanti ! Shanti ! Shantihi !

CHAPTER 32

Sagunameru Naik

Naik owned a shop at Shirdi. The devotees who came to Shirdi visited his shop for making purchases. One day, when a devotee named Madhuradas went to the shop, he found Naik and some others talking ill of a lady devotee who came to see Baba. Madhuradas also joined them in the in evil talk. When he came to Dwarakamai, Baba said to him, "What is Naik telling ? One must utilise the time given by God in a beneficial way and should not indulge in criticising others. All kinds of devotees come here, both good and bad. Why should you discuss about their character with others?"

Who is God?

One day a person from Kopargaon came to Baba and sought answers for his doubts. Baba wanted to know his doubts. Then the person asked, "Who is God? How will He be? Where will He be? How to see God?" Baba understood the mentality of the person and did not reply to him. Instead, he called a devotee and asked him to go to the marwari Chagchand and tell him that Baba wanted a loan of Rs.100. The devotee went to the marwari and came back empty-handed saying that the marwari told him he had no money and sent his salutations. Then Baba sent for Nana Chandorkar and asked for Rs.100. Since he had no money, Nana sent a written request to the same marwari Chagchand for a loan of Rs. 100. Nana received the amount immediately through the messenger. This he gave it to

Baba. The person who questioned Baba about God, asked Das Ganu as to why Baba, without answering his questions, was trying for a loan of Rs. 100. Das Ganu told him that Baba was doing all that for his sake. The marwari, while he declined to give loan to Baba, gave it readily to Nana Chandorkar. Similarly, if one wants to know about God, he should have the capacity to understand. Otherwise, he cannot understand whatever is said about God.

Samsara (Wordly Life) is Fearful

One's closeness to Baba was the result of good deeds over many births, and such a person was Nana Chandorkar. He learnt many things from Baba. He found this Samsara (Worldly life) to be like a fearful ocean. The *samsara* appeared to him like an obstacle for spiritual progress. He learnt this truth by practical experience. In the year 1918, one day when Baba was alone, Nana Chandorkar said to him, "Baba, I am finding the *samsara* very fearful. My mind is not interested in the worldly affairs. Somehow give me salvation from these attachments." On hearing this Baba smiled and said, "There is some truth in what you said. But the remaining is untruth and meaningless. You are under the impression that by taking to forests, one can escape from the trials and tribulations of the *samsara.* But this is not correct. It is only an illusion, because wherever you go, your body and mind are with you only. They will never leave you but will be giving you some kind of happiness. Our past actions are the basis for our present troubles and happiness. They should be faced courageously and with tact, and you should lead a family life in the proper way. By getting away from *samsara,* one cannot attain happiness. Everyone who proceeds in the spiritual way will have to face all these problems, and to think of *vairagya* (renunciation), as a solution, is not correct." This is the message of Sai Baba.

Pandaripur Lawyer

There was a lawyer Deshapande, at Pandaripur. The subjudge of this place was Noolkar, who was suffering from ill-health. He stayed at Shirdi for some days to get Baba's blessings. There was some discussion that one should take proper medicines for ill-health instead of going to fakirs. Deshpande partook in the discussions and he too blamed Sai Baba. He came to Shirdi many years after this incident. After touching the feet of Baba he sat in a corner of Dwarakamai. Baba turned towards, him and said, "People are cunning. They fall at the feet and give *dakshina,* but abuse behind his back." Deshpande understood to whom Baba intended his words. He was surprised as to how Baba could know about this which had happened some years before at Pandaripur which was 300 miles form Shirdi. He wondered at the omniscience of Baba. From that day he resolved not to talk ill of others and not to participate in such discussions. In this way Baba's *darshan* had put him in the right path.

Periods of Deeksha (Vow)

Baba used to give *deeksha* to the devotees who came to him. The *deekshas* were prescribed by Baba depending on the stages of the devotees, and during this period he moulded them. Baba prescribed *Brahmmacharya Deeksha* (celibacy) to Tatya. Hari Seetharam Dixit and Kaka Dixit were given nine months period of *Vanaprastha* (away from wife and children) at Shirdi. Baba prescribed four years *deeksha* period to Upasini Baba who left Shirdi without completing the *deeksha* period. Similarly, Baba used to prescribe *deeksha* periods for some to do *Parayana* of holy books, and to some to do *Nama Sankeertan* (chanting of Names). The devotees were very much benefited by the *deeksha* periods prescribed by Baba.

Khaparde's Son—Plague

Khaparde's wife with her son stayed at Shirdi for some days. While there the boy had an attack of bubonic plague.

She feared very much for his life. She talked to Dixit and Shama and wanted to take her son to a good doctor. But there was no allopathic doctor at Shirdi. She wanted to take him to their native place Amaravathi, but lacked courage to take him on such a long distance. She was weeping bitterly fearing what would happen to her son. Shama, consoling her, said that there was nothing to fear when Sai Baba was there and advised her to take her son to Baba and put him at his the feet.

That evening while Baba was on his way to Lendi Bagh, she ran towards him and fell at his feet, washing them with her tears. She became speechless because of her suffering and could not even get up. Noticing her condition, Baba lifted her up and said, "Mother, the sky is overcast with dark clouds. But shortly the clouds will disperse and the sky will become clear." So saying he lifted his kafni (shirt) and showed four egg-sized buboes. He told he how he would suffer for his real devotees. Who is more to us than Baba who takes on him the sufferings of his devotees. In two days, the boy regained complete health.

Breaking of Baba's Brick

Baba looked after the brick given by his Guru Venkusa more than his life. While sleeping he kept it under his head. While sitting he put the brick beside him and put one hand on it. He used to say that the brick was a form of his Guru.

It was the month of August in 1918. One Thursday, Abdul, who used to clean the lanterns and keep the mosque tidy, took the brick in his hand. It fell down and broke into two pieces. Baba, who came afterwards, saw it and bemoaned its loss. He cried, "It is not the brick that is broken but my fate is broken into pieces. This was my life's companion all these years. With it I always meditated on the self and it is equal to my life. It has left me today." Through this incident also Baba indirectly indicated his impending 'Nirvana'.

Shamshuddin Miya

Even prior to the above incident, in June 1918, Baba made some arrangements, according to Muslim customs, which are done previous to the death of a person. He sent Rs. 250 to Shamshuddin Miya, a Muslim fakir of Aurangabad, through Khasim, son of Bade Baba of Shirdi, and also sent a garland for arranging Moul, Qawali and Nyas. He then sent the following message: "On ninth day of the ninth month Allah would be taking away the lamp he lit. This is the grace of Allah." Next day when Khasim reached Aurangabad and met Shamshuddin, without his telling him, Shamshuddin told the contents of Baba's message. As per Baba's wish he arranged in the name of Baba recitation about Paigambar, drums were played for Muslim saints. He spent all the money sent by Baba by arranging feeding of all who were present. Next day Khasim and Shamshuddin went to the great Muslim saint, Banne Mia, and found him standing in a peculiar position. When anyone went near him, he got angry and scolded and hit them. Everyone was cautioned not to go near him. But Shamshuddin without fear went near him and after putting the garland sent by Baba around his neck, conveyed the message sent by him. On hearing the message Banne Miya wept, since Baba would be leaving his mortal body. The Ninth day of the ninth month in Urdu and Arabic calendars were equivalent to 15 October, 1918 *Ekadasi.*

To Die at Will

As all the above actions of Baba were in secrecy no one had any idea that he would leave his body soon. Therefore all the routine things went on as usual. Baba took good care in not creating any kind of suspision in his devotees about it. Only Dwarakamai, Gurudhan and Venkusa who were in an invisible form knew about Baba's 'Nirvana'. The devotees were worshipping Baba as usual.

The month of September came. The local merchants and those who came from outside Shirdi, were praying to Baba for more profits in their business. Baba was pained at the desire for money of such devotees. In the nights Baba used to discuss with Gurudhan, Dwarakamai and Venkusa the selfish desires of such devotees and the way they were pestering him. Since Sai Baba had no negative answers or actions in response to his devotees' prayers, he had to fulfil their desires at least to a certain extent, even though the recipients did not deserve it. If this went on like this, it would be against the laws of creation. Therefore, they decided that the only solution to this was that Baba should leave his body. Even taking into consideration the 83 years age of the body, it was time for leaving the body. Though Baba would leave his body, his power would be there. It was decided to spread sai Philosophy and to remove the *ajnana* (nescience) and blind beliefs in the people and make the people lead peaceful and happy lives. Towards this goal, they decided to fill this world with love for the next 500 years. They decided that Sai Baba might take another form according to the need and orders of God. Since Baba had the ability to lay down his life at his will, he was setting the time for his leaving the human body. The day was the 28th of September. The noon arathi was going on. One group of merchants from Bombay entered Dwarakamai. Baba felt pained on seeing them. The merchants came here after hoarding essential foodgrains in godowns with a prayer to Baba to see that they get double the rates. They brought with them large amounts of money to give Baba as *dakshina.* Having understood the purpose of their visit, Baba told those who were there that there would not be any *darshan* after arathi was over. The merchants approached Shama and Nana Chandorkar and pleaded with them for arranging an interview with Baba, as they had to return to Bombay urgently. Shama innocently took them inside Dwarakamai, convincing Baba. Seeing the situation, Baba understood that the time had come for him to leave the body. From that day Baba increased the temperature of his body which appeared as if he had fever. Unable to bear the mental suffering caused to him by the devotees, Baba wanted to lay down his life at will. He stopped taking food, thereby shrinking his body and to making his death appear like a natural one. Usually death comes due to ill-health, accidents or old age. But Sai Baba had to leave the body only for the sake of his devotees. In this way he who worked throughout his lifetime for his devotees, had to leave the mortal body at his will, for the sake of devotees only.

Om Shanti ! Shanti ! Shantihi !

CHAPTER 33

In the previous chapter we learnt how Baba suffered on account of the selfishness of some devotees, without his close devotees also not knowing about this. Disciples should not go against the wishes of their Guru, even in small matters. Sometimes they may do something out of love for their Guru, even though the Guru tells them not to do it. By doing such things they should know that they are making the Guru suffer. Unfaithfulness to one's Guru is the same as unfaithfulness to God, since Guru is God.

Tatya's health deteriorated from the end of July. Ramchander Patil was very much worried about this and was always looking after him. Knowing that Tatya's death was coming closer, Patil satisfied the tastes of Tatya. Poor Tatya did not know about his impending death ! Though he was suffering from ill health, he was cheerful. But Patil was suffering mentally. The month of August was gone and September came. By the end of September Tatya was bedridden. He could not even walk up to Dwarakamai. The tuberculosis from which Tatya was suffering advanced and everyone thought that he would not survive. But Tatya never bothered about his health. He was a single person, a bachelor. With his association with Baba, he lost his attachment to his body and thus he had no fear of death. He was always thinking about changing Baba's dress and arranging his bed in the nights in his absence.

Reading of Sacred Books

On the first of October, a Brahmin devotee, Vaje, came to Baba and saluted him with folded hands. Baba, while blessing him with *udi prasad,* noticed a book in his hands and asked him what book it was. Vaje said it was *Rama Vijayam* written by the poet Sreedhar. Baba took it and turned the inner pages several times. After that he asked Vaje to read that book aloud, seated near him. Vaje took Baba's orders as a great boon and commenced reading immediately. Now and then in the middle Baba would explain clearly certain matters contained in the book, for the benefit of the devotees who were there. This went on daily in the mornings and evenings. It was the practice to read sacred books before a person who would die soon. Baba kept this also a secret. The book was completely read by Vaje three times in a period of 14 days. Tatya's ailment was becoming serious day by day. He was vomiting blood. Everyone thought that his days are counted.

On 8 October 1918, Baba become very weak. He sat leaning on the wall of the mosque. Arthis and worship were done as usual. As he was very weak, the devotees were not allowed to go near him and this was ensured by Shama and Nana Chandorkar. Some people with a tiger in the cart were going round places and earning money. They came to Shirdi and brought the tiger near to Dwarakamai. The tiger was suffering from some disease and was weak. On seeing Baba, it stretched its two front legs and lay down. It appeared as if the tiger was saluting Baba. Baba looked into the eyes of the tiger for a long time. The tiger also looked at Baba and shed tears. Seeing Baba thus it breathed its last. There must have been a tie-up in one of its previous births with Baba. Thus Baba helped the tiger to merge with God.

Last Days

Even though Baba became very weak, he gave necessary directions to the devotees. He had taken a human form only to help the devotees. He never did anything for himself. His life's aim was to provide peace and happiness to all mankind. He worked towards this end, day and night. Even in the middle of the night he was in solitary meditation and saved many devotees at far and near places. The devotees who noticed Baba's ill-health and the shrinking of his body due to poor intake of food, thought this to be a strange act but they never thought that his life was ebbing. Bhagoji Shinde, Mhalsapathi, Abdul, Nana Chandorkar, Shama, Lakshmi Bai, Bhate, Dixit and others were looking after Baba day and night. With a view not to cause anxiety to his devotees, he would go up to Lendi Bagh and Butty Wada now and then. The Chavadi procession also was held as usual. Shama's uncle Laxman Mama cooperated with Jog in giving *arathis.* Butty and Dixit sat along with Baba and took food. In the absence of Baba, they were not able to relish their food. Baba as usual went out for alms to five houses and after collecting the food, put some in the Dhuni and fed the animals and birds with the remaining food.

Baba's body looked very weak. The eyes which were shining like fire, were sunken. Even then there was no change in his concentrated looks. He gave proper advice and *udi prasad* to the devotees who came to him. Das Ganu, with the permission of Baba, had gone to Pandaripur to fulfil certain engagements. From 13 October, Baba stopped going to Lendi Bagh and also for alms. He sat in Dwarakamai and gave courage to the devotees. He had been unwell once in 1916 and recovered. The devotees thought that Baba would recover this time also. But the close associates of Baba were very much worried over his not taking any food. Hence they stayed in the mosque thoughout the night looking after him. On the night of 14 October, even though he was seriously ill, he got up and made loud noise and hit the floor with his *sataka.* Everyone woke up at the sound. Then Baba explained his action by saying that thieves had come to Khaparde's house at Amaravathi and he drove them away. In his last hours also Baba was thinking about his devotees only and not about himself.

Final Day

The day was Tuesday, the 15th of October, 1918. It was the last day for Baba's physical body. The sun had risen as usual. That day was *Vijayadashami* (Dushera). Baba became bodily very weak. For ordinary persons, it would have been difficult even to get up and sit. But Baba got up as usual and sat in his place. Devotees came for his *darshan* as usual. Shama stopped some devotees from coming inside the mosque, as Baba was unwell and advised them to have *darshan* from outside. But Baba did not agree to this and asked all the devotees to come inside and have his *Pada darshan.* The devotees did so. Baba put his *Abhaya Hastha* on their heads, blessed them and gave them *udi prasad.* For unknown reasons, even the close devotees of Baba who were always with him, fell at his feet one after another. Baba gave them necessary advice as per their need. They took them as usual advice which Baba used to give, but failed to think that they were Baba's last ones to them while in physical body. Baba asked Laxman Mama, who was an astrologer and devotee, to do God's Namasmaran for some time.

The time was eleven in the morning. Tatya vomitted blood frequently and went into unconscious state. His pulse also became weak. Ramachander Patil and Bala Shimpe feared that Tatya will die that day as per Baba's prediction. They brought Shama and showed him the condition of Tatya. Thinking that Tatya would die in a few moments, Shama came running to Baba. He explained the condition of Tatya to Baba and prayed him to come to Tatya's house immediately and save him. Baba consoling Shama told him not to worry and assured him that Tatya would escape death as soon as Ekadasi set in that day. But Shama again requested Baba to come once and see Tatya. Then Baba told Shama, "All of you have the tie of friendship only with Tatya. But for me there is also the responsibility for his welfare. I gave word to his mother Baija Bai at the time of her death, that I would look after Tatya equal to my life. The service rendered by that mother and the word given by me to her cannot be forgotten. So you do not worry at all. To save Tatya I need not go there, and I can do it sitting here." After hearing this Shama calmed down.

The time was noon. Preparations were being made for noon *arathi.* It appeared as if some divine light entered Baba. *Arathi* was started. Throughout the *arathi* Baba's facial features were changing every moment. Those who looked at him had peace of mind and felt like looking at him continuously. During that period Baba appeared in different forms to the devotees present there. He appeared in the forms of Maruthi, Vittal, Dattatreya, Rama, and to Muslim devotees as Mecca and Medina. For one Christian devotee, he appeared as Jesus. For Butty he appeared as Sri Krishna playing the flute in the Wada built by him. One devotee brought his little son for initiating him to education by Baba, that being Vijayadashami day. To him Baba appeared as Vigneshwara and writing the sanskrit alphabet 'OM' showed it to the boy and blessed him. In this manner Baba, during *arathi* time that day, had shown his divine form to the devotees as per their thoughts.

Arathi was over. The time was one hour past noon. Baba ordered all the devotees to go away quickly. With joy at Baba's divine *darshan,* all of them went away to their houses and wadas. Suddenly Baba had a severe cough and he vomitted blood. There, Tatya recovered and his pulse came to normal. Some new strength entered his body. He stood up and could walk also. He cried out of joy. He could not understand from where he got this new energy all of a sudden. The onlookers were also surprised. Before he recovered from this surprise, he remembered Baba. Thinking that Baba had given him another lease of life, he went running to the mosque.

By that time Baba leaned on Baija Appaji Patil and was telling him something secretly. Saying this, he warned him not to reveal this to others, otherwise he would die. Tatya heard these last words. Baba was getting severe cough and was heaving. Whenever he coughed, blood poured out through his mouth and fell all over Dwarakamai. Beforehand Baba had asked his devotees to be without fear and sent them for their meals. But a few devotees refused to leave Baba. Lakshmi Bai, Bhagoji, Appaji, Laxman, Bala Shimpe were sitting near Baba. When Tatya saluted Baba, he asked Shama to take Tatya and leave him in his house. Shama returned after leaving Tatya in his house. The time was two o'clock in the afternoon. Baba sent away the others also for meals.

Charity of Nine Rupees

Lakshmi Bai Shinde and Bayyaji were the only ones remaining. She was near Baba's feet. Baba put his right hand in his shirt pocket twice, took out Rs. 5 and Rs. 4 and gave them as charity to Lakshmi Bai. Baba explained the significance of these nine rupees as the nine qualities a devotee should have: (1) Absence of egoism (2) Absence of jealousy (3) Untiring service (4) Absence of worldy desires (5) Complete faith in Guru (6) Peaceful nature (7) Desire to know the truth (8) Absence of envy, and (9) Absence of self-boasting and finding faults in others. Unless a devotee improved these nine qualities, he could not have true devotion to reach God. Thus Baba taught to Lakshmi Bai even in his last moments.

Baba's Mahasamadhi

Dashami ended and Ekadashi came. The time was 2.30 in the afternoon. Baba told Bayyaji that he was leaving this world and his body was to be kept in Butty Wada, assuring him that from there he would be protecting his devotees at all times. So saying Baba leaned on the body of Bayyaji. He did not fall on the floor, or his bed. He breathed his last giving charity and teaching *Jnana* to his children. This is the way the king of yogis—Yogiraja—attained *Samadhi*. Lord Shiva who is capable of commanding death, and who was born as human, invited death. The divine light which came out of the body of Baba, joined Gurudhan, Dwarakamai and Venkusa, who were already in the form of divine lights (jyotis) and all the four jyotis combined into one as Sai's divine power. It again divided into four parts. One part went to Gurusthan. The second part went to Chavadi and settled there. The third part merged in Dwarakamai and the fourth part went into Butty Wada. These four powers represent the four *Vedas.* These are the proofs of Sai Power which can command and control the whole world. The Shivashakti from Kailash came and stayed in Shirdi. In this way Shirdi became a holy place. The body of Sai who exhibited supernatural powers and saved several devotees, was lying in Dwarakamai.

The physical body of Sai Baba, lying in Dwarakamai, cannot be seen again. So let us imagine ourselves to be in Dwarakamai and touch the holy feet of Sai Baba and make our life meaningful.

Om Shanti ! Shanti ! Shantihi !

CHAPTER 34

The news of Baba's *Samadhi* spread throughout Shirdi and the neighbouring villages in minutes. People came along with women and children to Dwarakamai. They wept uncontrollably as Sai Baba, who was God to them, was no more. They became speechless when they saw the lifeless body of Sai Baba, and felt as if the entire world had come to standstill. There was not a single family either in Shirdi or the neighbouring places which had not experienced Baba's *leelas* and greatness. They cried loudly, recollecting the good things Baba had done to them. Some fell down unconscious after seeing Baba's body. Some were seen weeping and running in the streets. There is none who did not shed tears. They now understood the 'Seemollanghan' incident of two years back and how Baba had taken on himself Tatya's death and given his life to him. Several people were recollecting Baba's strange actions and words. Some said that Baba had indicated that he would born again after eight years, in Madras State. Some imagined that what Baba had told Appaji secretly must be about his future birth. Since he had warned Appaji not to reveal anything to others, he kept silent in spite of so many people questioning him.

After a few hours, the question as to what to do with Baba's mortal remains arose. Some Muslims requested that the body of Sai Baba may be kept in *Samadhi,* outside the mosque in the open space. Khushal Chand and Amir Shakkar also supported this. But the village munsif, Ramachander Patil, took a firm decision that Baba's

Samadhi should be in Butty Wada and nowhere else. This way two groups formed in Shirdi and began arguing over the matter. By Tuesday evening, the Sub-Inspector of Police from Rahata, Chakranarayan, came to Shirdi. When he searched Baba's body he found seven rupees in his pocket. The whole night discussions and arguments went on regarding the location of the *Samadhi.*

In the early hours before daybreak on Wednesday the 16th, Baba appeared to Das Ganu in his dream and told him that the mosque came down, and the merchants were angry with him, so he left his body. He asked him to proceed immediately to Shirdi and cover his body with jasmine flowers.

Das Ganu, along with his disciples, started for Shirdi immediately. Pradhan's wife at Bombay had a dream on the night of 15th. She dreamt that Baba's life was leaving his body and she cried that Baba was dying. Baba told her in the dream that one should not say dying in the case of saints, but say "attained *Samadhi*".

He again appeared in her dream on the 16th night and requested her to give him all the money she had in her box. Next day she sent all the money in her box to Shirdi for utilising for the last rites of Baba. The same night Baba appeared in the dream of Pradhan's sister and asked her to send silk clothes to put on his *samadhi.* She sent the clothes to Shirdi. In the early hours of Wednesday Baba appeared in the dream to Laxman Mama Joshi and said, "Bapu Saheb Jog is thinking that I am dead. I only left my body and I am alive. Get up and give Kakad *arathi.*" Laxman Mama who had full faith in Baba, went to the mosque taking with him the puja items required for Kakad *arathi.* Even though the police and village servants tried to prevent him from entering the mosque, he forcibly entered inside and gave Kakad *arathi* to Baba's body. Seeing his determination none could stop him. The noon *arathi* was given by Bapu Saheb Jog. This was the last *arathi* given in Dwarakamai.

On Wednesday morning the tahsildar of Kopargaon Taluk came and gathered the views of both the groups regarding the place of *Samadhi* and asked them to express their views in writing along with their signatures. The majority wanted that Baba should be laid to rest in Butty Wada. Even then, the tahsildar had no courage to take a decision but wanted to act according to the orders of the District Collector, Ahmednagar. But in the meantime, the other group reconciled to the situation and agreed for the *Samadhi* inside Butty Wada.

In the evening of Wednesday at about 4 o'clock they wanted to bathe the body of Baba. When they tried to remove the *kafni* (long shirt) the hand bent as usual. In ordinary cases the limbs cannot be bent as they stiffen. Baba's body was laid on a big table before Dwarakamai, and potfuls of water were poured on the body with devotion. After that they spread a white cloth on the body. They put flowers, sandal and *akshatas* (rice) over the cloth. For the last time everyone had the *darshan* of Baba's body to their hearts content. A grave, 6 feet in length, was dug in Butty Wada's underground structure, enough for keeping his body. The body was taken into Butty Wada in procession to the sounds of various musical instruments. First, the broken brick of Baba was broken into smaller pieces and put in the grave, over that soft beds were spread. Dixit, Butty, Shama and Mhalsapathi slowly lifted the body. The thought that in a few moments the body would be hidden from their view, gripped the devotees present there and all of them burst into tears. There was complete silence except for snifflings. Due to sadness, the devotees felt weak and all of them together could not lift Baba's body. A few of them got into the grave and from below caught the body and it was slowly lowered. The head side went down first. Someone cried aloud that Baba was going away. The devotees surrounding the grave tried to catch a glimpse of the body for the last time. The entire body was lowered and rested on the soft beds. Rose water and perfumes were sprayed on the body. When they started putting earth on the body, the people wept and rolled on the floor, crying. Even God, if He is born on this earth, has to be buried under the earth. This is a fact.

Samadhi Temple

Butty's life was blessed. The Wada built by him became Baba's *Samadhi.* At five o'clock in the evening, after the *Samadhi,* Bapu Saheb Jog and Laxman Mama gave *sandhya arathi* in Butty temple for the first time on 16 October 1918. From that day onwards till date, four *arathis* are given to Baba daily. Nanavalli, who was like Baba's life, watched the *Samadhi* from a distance. He stopped taking food from that day and died on the 13th day.

Das Ganu, after reaching Shirdi on Thursday morning, did *sankeertan* for two days near the *Samadhi* of Baba. In the name of Baba, he fed a large number of people. Baba Saheb Bhate and Upasini Baba of Sakori Ashram performed the last rites of Baba. Where Butty wanted to install the idol of Sri Krishna, Baba's *Samadhi* came up. This way Baba became Muralidhar. The Butty temple with Baba's *Samadhi* in it had become the holiest of the holy places, giving millions of devotees peace and happiness.

Om Shanti ! Shanti ! Shantihi !

End of Seventh Day's Parayana

EIGHTH DAY'S 'PARAYANA'—THURSDAY

CHAPTER 35

As told by Baba to Laxman Mama, Das Ganu and Pradhan's wife in their dreams on the next day of his *Samadhi,* he did not die. He only left the body. The divine Sai Power from that day till date is always alert, protecting the devotees. There are numerous incidents in support of this. Though Shirdi is the centre of the divine power of Sai Baba, the entire world is filled with this divine power. That is why Baba gives *sakshatkar* whenever and wherever his true devotees call him with devotion. In fact, the divine power of Sai is experienced more after *Samadhi* and there are several incidents to prove this fact. To think that Sai Baba of Shirdi died will be incorrect. He is alive even today. Some devotees may entertain doubts as to how to see Baba, how to hear his words and how to have his Grace, if he is alive. One with a pure heart should have complete faith in Baba. His *Life History* should be read with devotion frequently. From the moment a person wakes up in the morning, he should be informed of all the jobs to be done during that day. He must first offer to Baba what all are proposed to be enjoyed through the five senses. If Baba's photo is in the house, he should think that he is one of the family members and do all service to him as done to other members, only then will Baba definitely reside in the house. This is cent per cent true. Worship with pomp and show is not required. He should install Sai Baba in his heart and merge in him. For such pious devotees Baba will be a slave.

His love for his devotees is so great. Those who have experienced Sai's love and affection will not hesitate to offer their lives at the feet of Sai. His love cannot be explained in words. To imagine Sai's power, our intellect is not enough.

We should make Sai one of our family members and a guide in our life and offer him everything. We should keep away from envy, hatred, ego and attachments and be helpful to the poor and needy. Then Sai in Guru form will carry our burden and guide us on to the proper path to reach our life's goal. This was the aim of Sai's incarnation. The greatness of Sai is spreading day by day not only in our country but to all the corners of the world. The Sai Power will be there for the next 500 years and a universal family will be established without class, creed and nationality. Let Sai's Peaceful Empire be established.

Om Shanti ! Shanti ! Shantihi !

THE REWARD OF PARAYANA (PHALA SHRUTI)

The *Life History of Shirdi Sai Baba* is a book containing Baba's *leelas,* greatness and teachings. It is a book for devotional reading. Sai Baba's teachings are the principles enunciated in the *Vedas.* All the great things contained in the scriptures were narrated by Baba in the form of stories, which could be understood even by lay people. His life is a spiritual institution for us.

If anyone does devotional reading of Baba's *Life History* for relief from worldly problems or difficulties, they will find relief, depending on their degree of devotion. If *Pārayana* is done not for physical benefits but for spiritual progress, then this acts as a divine medicine. May Sai Baba, the love incarnate, bestow peace and happiness and protect them from all evil. May Sai give them *sadgati* (merger in God).

SARVE JANA SUKHINOBHAVANTHU !

LOKA SAMASTHA SUKHINOBHAVANTU

Om Shanti ! Shanti ! Shantihi !

MANGAL ARATHI

(Arathi with camphor should be given till the completion of the MANGAL ARATHI)

(The following is the transliteration of the MANGAL ARATHI from Telugu)

Kailasa Vasa Sai	-	Mangalam	
Venkusa Priya Sishya	-	Mangalam	"Kailasha"
Dwarakamai Sai	-	Mangalam	
Gurudhan Putra Sai	-	Mangalam	
Butty Mandira Vasa	-	Mangalam	
Sachidananda Sai	-	Mangalam	"Kailasha"
Shirdi Vasa Sai	-	Mangalam	
Mahimavatara Sai	-	Mangalam	
Sarva Vyapaka Sai	-	Mangalam	
Dhukka Nashaka Sai	-	Mangalam	"Kailasha"
Shakti Pradhata Sai	-	Mangalam	
Sukha Pradhata Sai	-	Mangalam	
Bhukti Pradhata Sai	-	Mangalam	
Mukti Pradhata Sai	-	Mangalam	"Kailasha"

Sarvam Sai Padarpanam

MANGALARATHI

The purport of the Telugu MANGAL ARATHI is given below in English

Oh Sai Baba! Obeisance to you!
Oh Sai! You are Lord Shiva;
Your are the beloved disciple of Venkusa;
You live in Dwarakamai;
You are the Child of Gurudhan (Ganga Bhavajya);
You dwell in Butty temple;
You are the truthful bliss — You dwell in Shirdi;
You are the greatest incarnation;
You are omnipresent;
You are the remover of the sufferings of devotees;
You are the giver of energy, happiness, food and finally Mukhti (liberation) —
Oh Sai Baba! Obeisance to you!

I lay down my all
at the feet of Sai Baba

SRI SHIRIDI SAIBABA SEVA ASHRAM

Central (Regd.) Trust

Founder President: Sri Ammula Sambasiva Rao

"GURUNILAYAM"

Repuru Village, Kakinada-533 006.

East Godavari Dist. Andhra Pradesh, India

Our Pujya Guruji Sri Ammula Sambasiva Rao, established the above Seva Ashram with an intention to spread Shirdi Sai philosophy among the general public. Accordingly, he is performing Sai activities as under. The figures mentioned herein are based, as on 01--04-2002.

A. 1. **Samuhic Shirdi Sai Sathyavrathams**

(a) Common, special Sai Baba pooja with simple pooja materials and duration of 2 to 3 hours time.

(b) More than 50,000 of such Sathyavrathams have been performed by Guruji and his team.

2. **"Sri Sai" Saikoti Namalikhita Mahayagnams**

Starting with printing and distribution of books freely, to be written by the devotees as "Sri Sai" and collecting them from the devotees. This *yagna* consists of five parts:

(a) Performing the Sathyavrathams by keeping 2 crores "Sri Sai" namams at the Lotus feet of Sri Shirdi Sai Baba.

(b) Take out procession of these 2 crores Sai namams in the streets of the village/town/cities.

(c) Performing 12 hours chanting of "Om Sai, Sri Sai, Jaya Jaya Sai", by keeping 2 crores namams at the lotus feet of Sri Shirdi Sai Baba.

(d) Keeping these 2 crores namams in specially constructed sthupam by all devotees.

(e) Conducting "satsang" (discources) by Sai devotees & finally by Saiguru.

(f) 380 such mahayagnams have been done so far by Guruji and his team, thereby submitting installation of 760 crores of "Sri Sai" namams in different Sai Baba temples of the country.

3. **Installation (*prana prathis ta*) of Sri Shirdi Sai Baba statues in temples, as per Indian tradition and customs**

(a) Usually consisting of two and a half day programme.

(b) 180 of such Shirdi Sai Baba marble statues have been done by our Guruji and his team.

4. **Free marriages**
   (a) Free of cost and explaining the concept of marriage in detail, to have a peaceful married life.
   (b) 40 such marriages have been done in the above-mentioned yagnam etc.
5. **Conducting adhyatmic training classes for the different age groups**
   (a) The basics of life and precautions to be taken at different ages starting from childhood till the death of a person, explained in detail with notes in these classes, usually consisting of 2 days duration.
   (b) Such classes of 60 members in number, have been conducted so far at different parts of Andhra Pradesh, by educating the basics and goal of ordinary human life to around 5000 persons.
6. **Conducting Shirdi Sai Satsang speeches**
   (a) Applying Shirdi Sai miracles and teachings in our individual life and also how they are useful to a modern person to be peaceful in their materialistic and adhyatmic lives.
   (b) Such special speeches will also be organised in high schools and colleges.
   (c) Around 3000 such satsang speeches are conducted by Guruji and his team.
7. **Developing "Sai Sevaks"**
   (a) Every year, by conducting 9-day classes at different Ashram sites, 3 days each at one sitting and every sitting will have preliminary test. Only selected persons in the test will be allowed to participate in the second sitting and likewise in third sitting. Finally, selected Shirdi Sai devotees will be given lifelong Sai Sevak *deekshas*.
   (b) 345 such Sai sevaks have taken their lifelong *deekshas* from our Guruji so far and this will continue every year. Any Shirdi Sai devotee, from any country in the world, can participate in these classes and can take *deekshas* after processing 3 classes of 9 days.

All the above seven activities are done by our Pujya Guruji at free of cost basis, but the organisers have to bear to and fro fares with minium living facilities. The organisers have to bear the other expenses for performing the Shirdi Sai activities. These activities are done mainly with an intention to spread Sai philosophy amongst the general public in nook and corners of India, and propose to do these activities any where in the world.

B. 11 Telugu books and 3 English books are written by Guruji so far on Shirdi Sai philosophy. 9 different Telugu books are written by other Sai devotees of Guruji, on Shirdi Sai & Guruji's philosophy. There are 15 Telugu & one English audio cassettes & some video cassettes educating Sai philosophy of songs & speeches, satsang etc.

SAI SEVAK (298 in number)

C. As per our Pujya Guruji's words, all the four above "Sai Gurus" are equal to our Pujya Guruji Sri Ammula Sambasiva Rao, in discharging and spreading the Sai philosophy among the general public. They are capable of performing all the activities which are done by our Pujya Guruji, as mentioned above, and also any other activity connected with Shirdi Sai movements.

D. Our Pujya Guruji shifted his residence to Kakinada Ashram from Hyderabad on 19th April 2001, since a residence of Gurunilayam was being constructed separately for him in that Ashram. Interested persons, who require the assistance of our Guruji in performing Shirdi Sai activities, may contact directly, at the below mentioned address, our Guruji Sri Ammula Sambasiva Rao, to enable him to send any one of Saigurus Purohiths/ Sevaks etc. to perform the Sai activity at respective places, either in India or any country in the world.

E. Any further clarifications on the above matters can be acquired from–

Sri Ammula Sambasiva Rao **"Gurunilayam"** E-mail: gamorai@dh1.vsnl.net.in Only for other country's Sai Devotees	TRUSTEES SRI SHIRIDI SAIBABA SEVA ASHRAM CENTRAL TRUST REPURU, KAKINADA - 533 006.

Sterling Books on :

Sri Shirdi Sai Baba

1. SRI SAI SATCHARITA ENGLISH
The Life and Teachings of Shirdi Sai Baba
Govind R. Dabholkar (Hemadpant) Deluxe Edition : Rs. 500.00
Translated by : Indira Kher Paperback : 300.00
ISBN 81 207 2211 6

2. SAI BABA : HIS DIVINE GLIMPSES
V. B. Kher, Foreword by M. V. Kamath
ISBN 81 207 2291 4 95.00

3. SRI SAI BABA'S TEACHING AND PHILOSOPHY
Lt. Col. M. B. Nimbalkar
ISBN 81 207 2364 3 75.00

4. SHIRDI SAI BABA AND OTHER PERFECT MASTERS
C. B. Satpathy
ISBN 81 207 2384 8 135.00

5. A Solemn Pledge From
TRUE TALES OF SHIRDI SAI BABA (37 Colour Plates)
Prof. Dr. B. H. Briz-Kishore, F.I.E.
ISBN 81 207 2240 X 95.00

6. GOD WHO WALKED ON EARTH
The Life & Times of Shirdi Sai Baba
Rangaswami Parthasarathy
ISBN 81 207 1809 7 95.00

7. SRI SHIRDI SAI BABA
The Universal Master
S. P. Ruhela
ISBN 81 207 1664 8 65.00

8. SRI SAI BABA
Swami Sai Sharan Anand, Translated by V. B. Kher
ISBN 81 207 1950 6 125.00

9. LIFE HISTORY OF SHIRDI SAI BABA
Ammula Sambasiva Rao
ISBN 81 207 2033 4 95.00

10. SRI SHIRDI SAI BABA IN PICTURE
Gaurav K. Ghai 10.00

11. APOSTLE OF LOVE
Saint Saipadanada
Rangaswami Parthasarathy
ISBN 81 207 1923 9 150.00

12. IN SEARCH OF TRUTH
Ammula Samabasiva Rao
ISBN 81 207 2407 0 35.00

13. SRI SHIRDI SAI BABA POSTER
ISBN 81 207 2343 0 60.00
Size: 18.2 x 22.8, Laminated Both Sides

14. Unravelling The Enigma
SHIRDI SAI BABA IN THE LIGHT OF SUFISM
Marianne Warren 375.00

<u>*Hindi*</u>

15. पृथ्वी पर अवतरित भगवान: शिरडी के साई बाबा
रंगास्वामी पारसाथी
ISBN 81 207 2101 2 95.00

16. स्वप्न तथा सच्चाईयाँ भगवान के समक्ष
डा. नरेश भाटिया
ISBN 81 207 2075 X

17. सत्यसाई अवतार
आर. मोहन राय
ISBN 81 207 2142 X 90.00

Eleven Solemn Promises as Pledged by Baba for material success, Prosperity & Happiness.

1. Whoever comes to My abode, their suffering would come to an end once and for all.
2. The helpless would experience plenty of joy, happiness and fulfilment as soon as they climb the steps of My *mandir*.
3. I am ever vigilant to help and guide all those who come to Me, who surrender to Me and who seek refuge in Me.
4. There shall be no dearth of any kind in the houses of My devotees and I shall fulfil all their wishes.
5. If you look to Me I shall look to you and take care of all your needs.
6. If you seek My advice and help they shall be given to you at once.
7. If you cast your burdens on Me, I shall surely take them on and relieve you of them.
8. I shall be ever active and vigorous even after casting away My body.
9. I shall respond and act in human form and continue My work to My devotees from My *samadhi*.
10. My mortal remains shall speak, execute and discharge all the needs of My devotees.
11. My tomb shall bless, speak and fulfil innumerable needs of My devotees.